Living with Plants

Living with Plants

A Guide to Indoor Gardening

Sophie Lee

Photography by Leonie Freeman

hardie grant books

CONTENTS

ABOUT GEO-FLEUR

Hello! I'm Sophie Lee, founder of botanical styling company geo-fleur. I love adding greenery to everything, whether it's a windowsill, bookcase or even a bedpost. Plants make everything feel and look more beautiful, no matter how big (or small) the space. At geo-fleur, along with educating our customers about the joys of indoor gardening, we aim to inspire everyone to green up their homes.

I started geo-fleur back in October 2014, but I have always had an obsession with house plants; my mum is a florist (and a huge inspiration!) and from a young age I was always helping her out with making occasion buttonholes, big table decorations and bridal bouquets. I guess green fingers run in the family, as my uncle is the head gardener of a National Trust garden and goes seed collecting in Japan – he would always bring me back the most beautiful succulents to propagate, which then prompted me to start my own company. This is why succulents feature so much at geo-fleur!

My business partner, Sally, prefers plants without flowers, so when she got married I suggested that I plant her up a terrarium to carry down the aisle. It all kind of took off from there; I made a few more and then got addicted, and now run my own terrarium workshop so people can learn how to make their own miniature landscapes. For me, terrariums are the perfect example of indoor gardening, and how you can bring the beauty of nature into your home.

Indoor plants can be just as good as an outdoor garden – plus, they are versatile, personal and can move house when you do! Plants can add subtle pops of green to a room, or serve as a dramatic focal point. Whether your style is modern and minimal or vintage and whimsical, you can find the right plant to suit you. Once you start a plant collection, you won't be able to stop – you'll soon be giving them names and treating them to fancy, decorative pots.

Not just for show, plants are hugely beneficial to your health. Studies have proved that house plants improve concentration, purify the air, improve productivity, lower blood pressure and boost your mood. They serve a practical and aesthetic purpose, and will enhance your life.

As well as plant styling tips, I have also included some helpful How To ideas, to help you create bespoke, plant-based decor for your home. The demand for indoor plants and ways to display them only grows, and I can't wait to share my knowledge with everyone out there who wants to create their own indoor jungle. I hope you'll find this book insightful and that it will inspire you to get creative with nature and make your own green, urban sanctuary.

THE BEAUTY OF PLANTS

Plants are an easy and stylish way to bring energy into your
home and transform its look. They come in all kinds of shapes,
sizes and textures to suit your taste and space.

In many cities, outdoor space and gardens are at such a premium. It's no wonder geo-fleur has flourished selling weird house plants and cacti, as there is such a trend for house plants and adding some greenery to your indoor space. It's so tempting to run out and buy a huge collection straight away, but once you have purchased your beautiful plants, you need to know how to care for them. That's where I can help. This book will be your plant bible; it will help you find the right plants for your home and how to care for them correctly, teaching you all the tips and tricks to help your indoor garden to thrive.

Health benefits of keeping plants in your home

House plants are good for your health: they release oxygen into your home, control humidity and purify the air. An indoor garden can be your sanctuary from the outside world, and for many people it is a source of great joy. Whether you live in a small apartment, or a large country house, by introducing certain plants into your home, you will start to notice improvements to your health, and overall happiness.

Knowing what plants are best for what room is crucial when it comes to plant styling: the bathroom is perfect for air plants and kokedama, as the excess moisture from your daily shower helps those particular plants flourish. If you're lucky enough to have a conservatory or a super hot room, then fill it with ferns, palms, succulents and cacti as they will love the heat. Most plants don't like direct midday sun, so please be wary of this when placing your plants in your home. The biggest killer for house plants is overwatering and accidentally drowning them! See pages 124–127 to learn how to correctly water your plants.

It is so easy to add some greenery to your home, and you will notice an instant change. Adorn your windowsills with succulents, drape vibrant macramé hangers from curtain rails or try something big and bold like the gorgeous fiddle leaf fig. You can also have fun with the pots, and display your plants in beautiful ceramic and copper containers. Owning plants doesn't have to be expensive: just take a cutting from a friend's plant or from your local plant shop. There is also a section on this book for beginner's plants and how to style your home with a few statement, hardy plants (page 49).

I hope that by reading this book, you will develop a knowledge of how to care for and grow your own indoor plant collection, and share this knowledge with friends to help their collection grow too!

MAKE A MARBLED PLANT POT

You can use a new or old terracotta plant pot for this How To, but I find that using an old one just adds to the texture and charm. Make sure that the pot is clean and unglazed or the inks will not stick. At geo-fleur we use Scola iridescent inks, but there are many different marbling inks on the market. You can also marble a matching terracotta saucer for your pot to stand in.

3–4 different coloured marbling inks

large bucket filled with clean water

a stick

unglazed terracotta plant pot

rubber gloves (optional – I like to get messy!)

newspaper or plastic sheet

paint brush

sealant

plant of choice

1. Drip a couple of drops of each of your chosen colours of marbling ink into the bucket of water, then use a stick to swirl the inks around.

2. Hold the pot on its side and place it in the water, keeping your hand steady to avoid twisting the pot. Then, again without twisting the pot, lift it all the way out of the water. Feel free to wear rubber gloves for this part (but I prefer to get messy!).

3. Repeat the process of submerging and lifting. You can change the water at this point and add different inks to get a variety of vivid colours on the pot.

4. Keep dipping the pot into the water until the whole surface is covered and you are happy with the pattern – remember to not twist or dunk it completely as this will disturb the pattern.

5. Stand the pot upright on some newspaper or plastic sheeting to protect the surface from the ink. Leave it to dry for at least 3 hours for the marble ink to set.

6. Using a paint brush, coat the dry pot with sealant to protect the plant from any toxins in the marbling inks. Leave the sealant to dry completely (about 2 hours).

7. Once the sealant is dry, pot up your favourite plant and display with pride!

Tag your finished #LivingWithPlantsMarbledPot #LivingWithPlantsHowTo @geo_fleur

CHAPTER ONE

GETTING
STARTED

If you're lucky enough to have the space, large plants, such as the Monstera deliciosa *(Swiss cheese plant) make a stunning architectural feature.*

PICKING THE RIGHT PLANTS FOR YOU & YOUR HOME

So you have decided to make the commitment to embark on the indoor plant wagon. First of all, stand back and look at each of your rooms. Then answer the following questions: How much space do you have? Do you want to go for a jungle style or something more minimal? What are the light levels like? Do you have hanging space, room on a cabinet for a few pots, or a whole bookcase that needs jazzing up with plants?

It is important to think about what size plants will best suit your space – will several small potted plants fit better or just one large statement plant? Big plants need enough room to encourage their sculptural quality and architectural form, so there is no point dwarfing them in a small space.

Large plants look great in contemporary, open-plan areas with clean lines and minimalist décor. However, if your home is more crowded and bursting with personality I would recommend investing in some smaller plants to add character.

If you are totally new to keeping plants, it is a good idea to start with a few small and medium-sized pots containing hardy, low-maintenance plants (page 49). You will soon experience that joyous moment when a new leaf comes through on your plant.

I will guide you on which types of plant look great in which containers, as well as combinations you should avoid. As a rough guide, a two-thirds to one-third proportion works well. With a large pot, two-thirds should be plant and one-third container. But you do not have to stick to this rule and with practice you can manipulate scale and proportion to great effect. Large containers can look striking when filled with low-growing textural plants, such as *Maranta leuconeura* (prayer plant), making a feature of the pot. However, if you go for smaller plants that spill over the edges of the container, interest is focused on the plants.

Paint a wall in a bright colour or use a jazzy wallpaper and place a structural plant in front. Instant gratification.

Along with using pots, I will show you some different ways to style your home with plants, such as creating a terrarium (pages 116–119 and 134–137), hanging kokedama moss balls (pages 78–81), or making a macramé plant hanger to suspend your trailing plants from the ceiling (pages 34–39). You need to be careful that the plant and container are in keeping with the style of each room, so that your indoor garden enhances your interior.

Bookcases and shelves are a great place to add some greenery. Place a few trailing plants among your favourite books, such as a *Ceropegia woodii* (string of hearts) or a *Philodendron scandens* (heartleaf philodendron). A coffee table or low-level shelving unit can become the centre of attention with a striking plant or a collection of different succulents placed on top. I believe that plants look best grouped together in odd numbers, but if you are into minimalism, an even number of plants arranged in a grid or geometric shape works brilliantly to create a very structured, organised effect. The choice is yours!

The celebrated German architect Mies van der Rohe famously declared that less is more; this does not apply with plants. More is more, and you will soon become addicted to caring for your plant collection. A key way to pick out different plants that look good together is to find different shapes and textures that complement each other. If you are finishing an interior, the plants you choose should be compatible with the space you are putting them into. There is no point placing a huge *Monstera deliciosa* (Swiss cheese plant) in a tiny bathroom: it just won't look right! It should be given enough space to showcase its dramatic sculptural appearance. Don't be afraid to try out placing your plants in a few different locations around the house to see where they look best.

Many common house plants are prized for their wonderful leaves, which almost look as if they are made of painted silk. This is what makes the magical world of plants so interesting: their different shapes, their spots, pleats, hairs, spikes and grooves. As well as considering the space you want to put your plants in, think about whether you want colourful leaves, such as a *Calathea roseopicta* (rose-painted calathea), or something simple and striking like a *Pilea peperomioides* (Chinese money plant).

Some plants need more care than others, so once you have established whether you are going for sculptural large plants or miniature pots of cacti, you need to determine the level of maintenance you will be able to commit to. As well as the aesthetics of the room you want to keep plants in, you also need to consider the environmental conditions. Some plants need lots of light (see page 47 for more information on light levels), others more humidity. Your goal is to simulate a plant's native environment in order for it to flourish.

Plants need six key nutrients to survive: carbon, hydrogen and oxygen (which they get from water and air) and nitrogen, phosphorous and potassium, which come from their growing medium and so you will need to provide. When grown in the ground, these last three elements are naturally replenished, but because our plants will live in pots we need to manually top them up with fertiliser as the plant uses up the nutrients. I recommend using an organic fertiliser, which will not only feed the plant but also the soil.

• *Monstera deliciosa*
(Swiss cheese plant)

Asparagus setaceus *is most commonly known as the asparagus fern, but is not actually a fern at all – it's a climbing evergreen herb.*

• *Bromeliaceae* (Bromeliad)

• *Davallia* (Hare's foot fern)

• *Asparagus setaceus* (Asparagus fern)

• *Hevea brasiliensis* (Rubber tree)

Platycerium (Staghorn fern)

Pilea peperomioides (Chinese money plant)

• *Nephrolepis* (Boston fern)

• *Ficus lyrata* (Fiddle leaf fig)

To maximise your space, make a feature of your bookcase or bedpost by adding a few ferns or some striking air plants.

Windowsills and table tops are great places to add different plants of all sizes. Choose a combination of textures and colours for maximum impact.

Brighten your windows with a macramé plant hanger (pages 34–39). They are easy to make and are the perfect accessory to dress your home.

Eight Golden Rules to Start You off on Your Plant Journey

1. Do not drown them: Overwatering is the most common killer for indoor house plants. Find out how to properly water your plants on pages 124–127.

2. Let them rest: People are usually surprised to learn that nearly all plants need a rest period, which is usually in winter. During this time, you need to water them and feed them less, and let them be a little cooler.

3. Give them extra humidity: When keeping indoor plants, your central heating and other heat sources can make the air very dry. It is important to increase air humidity by misting your plants – learn how on page 123.

4. Watch out for plant trouble: Whether you are an expert or a beginner, there will be times when your plants will experience some trouble. One or two small insects or pests can be removed easily, but if you get an infestation I'm afraid that it is game over. Overwatering isn't fatal at first, but if you continue to do it, it will kill the plant. Watch out for the first signs your plant is in trouble (pages 128–131) and stop watering immediately.

5. Plants like to be together: You will have seen the trend of arranging all your plants together for a plant party. Nearly all plants grow better when they have their friends around them. #plantgang

6. Repotting is a skill you need to learn now: Some plants are slow-growing, whereas others you will have to run to catch up with their growth spurts. Learn to repot now, before your collection overgrows your home (pages 108–113).

7. Choose your plants wisely: Sadly, it is impossible to keep a beautiful, rare plant that only survives at perfect jungle temperatures in a cold, small flat. Even if you are a total expert, you cannot make a shade-loving plant survive in a sunny window.

8. Invest in some tools: A plant mister is a must, as you can easily water your plants by misting them and at the same time increase the humidity and reduce dust. Drip trays are great for watering your plants from the bottom, and some good-quality fertiliser will keep your plants looking healthy.

Step ladders are an easy and stylish way to showcase your plant collection. Place larger, leafier plants at the top and small cacti and succulents at the bottom.

The striking and vibrant rubber tree plant is also known as Ficus elastica. They can grow up to 15 m (50 ft) tall!

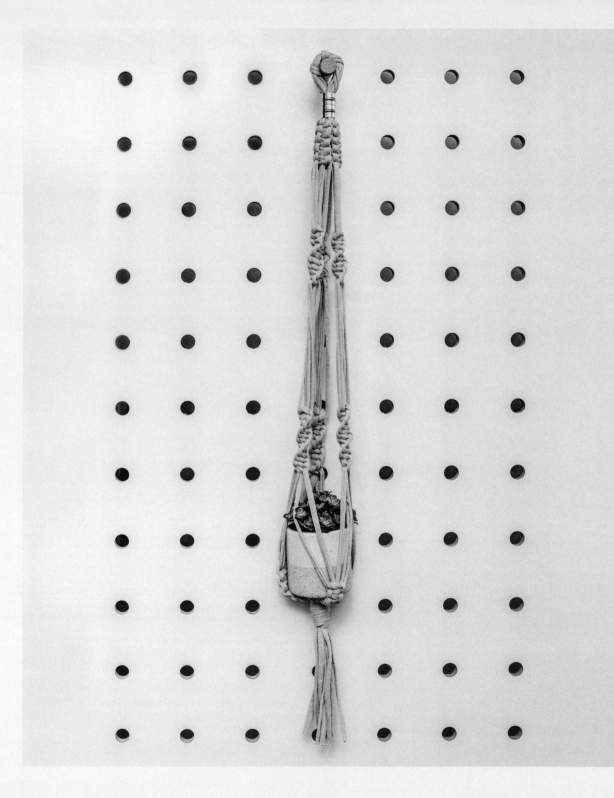

MAKE A MACRAMÉ PLANT HANGER

Macramé plant hangers were a huge trend in the 70s, and now they're making a comeback in a big way. They are great for elevating plants if you start to run out of shelf or floor space and make a wonderful feature in any room. Macramé and knitted wall hangers are a fun and easy way to add colour and texture to your home. As the plant grows, it will cascade beautifully over the hanger.

6 × 3 m- (10 ft 4½ in-) long pieces of cotton twine or
    recycled T-shirt jersey wool
copper straight coupler plumbing fitting
1 × 15 cm- (6 in-) long piece of cotton twine or
    recycled T-shirt jersey wool
ruler
scissors
S hook

1. Lay out the 6 long pieces of twine or wool so that they are side by side. Pick up the bunch and fold it in half so that you now have 12 lengths of twine. Push the folded end through the copper straight coupler until it comes through the other side to form a loop; at the other end of the coupler you should have 12 loose strands of twine.

2. Thread the 15 cm (6 in) piece of twine or wool up through the copper coupler until about half of it is at the same end as the loop. Wrap it around the loop several times to ensure the loop cannot be pulled back through the coupler. Thread the end back under the copper coupler to hide it.

3. Divide the twine into 3 groups of 4 strands. Each group of 4 strands is made up of 'working' strands (the 2 outside strands) and 'filler' strands (the 2 middle strands).

4. Make a square knot by taking the right-hand working strand and bringing it over the top of the 2 filler strands and underneath the left-hand strand. Bring the left-hand working strand behind both the right-hand strand and the filler strands, and up through the loop formed by the right-hand strand and the filler strands. Pull on both strands to tighten and push this half of the knot up to the copper coupler. To complete the square knot, you simply need to repeat these steps but in reverse: take the left-hand working strand and place it over the top of the two filler strands and underneath the right-hand strand. Bring the right-hand working strand behind both the left-hand strand and the filler strands and up through the loop formed by the left-hand strand and the filler strand. Pull on both strands to tighten and push up to the first knot.

5. Repeat this process, until you have 7 tight square knots in a row. Repeat for the other 2 groups of strands.

6. Starting with the first group of strands, measure a 7 cm (2¾ in) gap using a ruler or 4 fingers.

7. Beneath this gap, create a half-knot spiral by taking the right-hand working strand and placing it over the top of the 2 filler strands and underneath the left-hand strand. Bring the left-hand working strand behind both the right-hand strand and the filler strands, and up through the loop

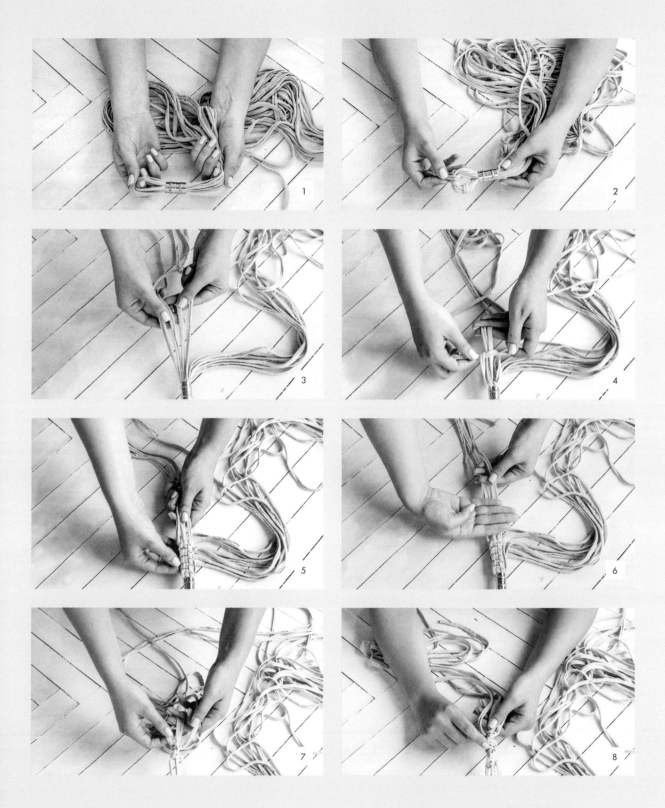

formed by the right-hand strand and the filler strand. Pull on both strands to tighten.

8. Tie a further 6 half-knot spirals onto the same group of strands by repeating step 7 until you have a spiral made up of 7 half-knots.

9. Tie 7 half-knot spirals on to the other 2 groups of strands.

10. Start the process again with the first group of strands and leave another 7 cm (2¾ in) gap. Tie another 7 half-knot spirals and repeat this process on the remaining 2 group of strands.

11. Regroup the strands into new groups of 4 by taking the 2 right-hand strands from one group and adding them to the 2 left-hand strands from the adjoining group.

12. Starting 5 cm (2 in) down one of these new groups of strands, work 4 square knots on to the group of strands by repeating step 4.

13. Repeat step 11, followed by step 4, for the remaining 2 groups of strands.

14. Cut a 50 cm (1 ft 7½ in) length from one of the longer excess twine lengths making sure you leave enough twine for the tassel.

15. Using the separate piece of twine you have just cut off, tie a gathering knot around the whole bunch of 12 strands directly underneath the rows of 4 square knots. To make a gathering knot, create a loop at one end of the separate piece by folding it over about 10 cm (4 in) from one end. Lay the loop on top of the bunch of strands, under the end of the row of square knots, so that the loop is at the bottom and the 2 loose pieces of the loop are over the square knots – 1 long piece and 1 shorter 'tail'. Wind the long piece tightly around and down the bunch of strands and the loop 6 or 7 times towards the bottom of the loop. Thread the end of the twine through the loop and pull on the upper strand 'tail' until the loop at the bottom disappears inside the wrapped twine section.

16. Trim all the remaining lengths of twine to create a tassel.

Tag your finished #LivingWithPlantsMacrame #LivingWithPlantsHowTo @geo_fleur.

CHAPTER TWO

CHOOSING THE RIGHT PLANT

SELECTING HEALTHY PLANTS

When buying a house plant, it is important that you take the time to check if it is healthy to ensure it will be happy once you have got it home. There is nothing worse than missing a telltale sign of underwatering or overwatering, and then discovering your plant only has a couple of weeks of life left. See page 49 to help you make the right decision when picking your plants.

You can buy plants in various sizes and stages of growth, but if you buy from a garden centre you will find that a lot of plants are sold in small pots. These are young plants that have been potted up from seed or cuttings so you need to take particular care to choose one that is healthy to give it the best chance of growing on for years to come.

Some types of plant are much more expensive than others due to being rare specimens: they grow more slowly or are difficult to propagate. There is a huge selection of plants on the market and the different prices and shapes can be bewildering. Some small bonsai trees can be very expensive, as they may be 60 years old. However, a 2 metre- (6½ feet-) tall *Chamaedorea elegans* (parlour palm) could be half that price as they are relatively fast-growing and easy to propagate.

If you want lots of greenery and volume, but money is limited, buy small, compatible plants, which can be grouped together to create immediate impact. Another easy way to grow plants cheaply is to ask friends and family if you can take cuttings from their plants. I'm constantly 'borrowing' cuttings from my mum's greenhouse, as she seems to have a magic touch with plants.

Tips To Check For A Healthy Plant

> Strong healthy leaves
> Firm stem
> No insects or pests anywhere on the plant (remember to check on the underside of leaves and along the plant's stem as many pests will hide or be camouflaged)

Succulents are perfect first plants as they are low maintenance, easy to propagate and suited to most homes. They are best placed on the windowsill where they can get the most sunlight.

LIGHT & SHADE

Different plants need different levels of sunlight in order to survive; some love getting as much sun as possible, whereas others prefer cooler, shady spots. It is important to work out how much, or little, sunlight a plant will be exposed to in each room. A sun-loving plant will not survive in a dark corner, and a shade-dwelling plant will struggle in full sun. Once you have established the light levels in your rooms you can choose the best plants accordingly.

North-facing windows

Rooms with north-facing windows get no direct sunlight at all, and will be the shadiest and coolest rooms in the house. There are plenty of plants that love this environment and will thrive when grown here. *Hedera helix* (common ivy) looks beautiful trailing down a bookcase and the *Sansevieria trifasciata* (snake plant) makes a striking feature.

East-facing windows

Rooms with an east-facing window will get direct sunlight from dawn until about mid-morning to noon, depending on the time of year. Early morning sun is less harsh than the afternoon sun, so east-facing rooms are perfect for plants that like a gentle amount of light and heat, but will also enjoy some time in the shade

once the sun has moved on. Try a *Pilea peperomioides* (Chinese money plant) here. In the more shielded parts of the room, you can also grow plants that require full shade.

South-facing windows

South-facing windows allow sunlight into the room throughout the day, including during the hottest early to mid-afternoon hours when the sun is closest to earth. Sun-loving and drought-tolerant plants flourish in these conditions, and leafy varieties tend to be fast-growing due to their prolonged exposure to sunlight. Succulents will thrive in full sun, and cacti like aloe add interest to a space while also being low maintenance.

West-facing windows

As with east-facing windows, rooms with west-facing windows only get direct sun for part of the day, but this time it is the later part. From early to mid-afternoon, sunlight will start to enter the room and will continue until dusk. However, because the room has already warmed up from the heat of the day, once the afternoon sun streams in it is usually much warmer than an east-facing room. In summer months it can get quite hot in west-facing rooms so plants that can tolerate heat are best in here. Try a *Fittonia* (nerve plant) or a Haworthia.

Easy-going plants for beginners

If you are new to gardening, here is a selection of plants that will suit you perfectly. All will provide you with lots of greenery, are easy to look after and are reasonably priced.

Monstera deliciosa (Swiss cheese plant): It is fairly inexpensive to buy a 30 cm (12 in) Monstera and it grows quickly, so you could get some easy height and beautiful leaves in under 3 months.

Epipremnum aureum (golden pothos or devil's ivy): This is a great group of plants to get started with as they are relatively low maintenance. The trailing varieties sprout new leaves regularly and are great in a hanging planter such as a macramé hanger. However, they are toxic to cats and dogs.

Hedera (ivy): Ivy is almost indestructible and has a good tell-tale sign when it needs watering as the leaves will look limp and soft.

Chlorophytum comosum (spider plant): These are great low maintenance plants, which need watering from the bottom perhaps once a week and a misting every now and then. They sprout babies regularly, off the end of their leaves, that are easy to propagate; you will be inundated with baby plants, which you can then share with friends and family.

AIR-PURIFYING PLANTS

In 1989, NASA conducted a study and found that some common house plants filter toxins from the air. The University of Technology Sydney also conducted research in 2013 which found that having plants in your workspace can be productive to your working day. Even with just one plant on your desk, you could find that you achieve a 37 per cent reduction in tension, 44 per cent reduction in anger and 38 per cent reduction in fatigue. Put these plants in your office to help you relax or your bedroom to help you sleep soundly.

My favourite NASA-approved air-cleansing plants are:

> *Nephrolepsis exaltata* (Boston fern)
> *Chlorophytum comosum* (spider fern)
> *Ficus benjamina* (weeping fig)
> *Spathiphyllum* 'Mauna Loa' (peace lily)
> *Sansevieria trifasciata* 'Laurentii' (variegated snake plant)
> *Dracaena fragrans* (corn plant)
> *Hedera helix* (common ivy)

BONSAI

I know what you are thinking: bonsai trees are not cool. But when you learn more about them you will be hooked, just like me. The traditional bonsai are now a little dated, but I'm trying for a resurgence.

There are records of bonsai trees dating from the early 14th century. The Chinese first began repotting naturally dwarfed trees from mountainsides into ornamental containers, appreciating the weird, twisted beauty of these mini trees in their homes. However, it is the Japanese who are responsible for cultivating bonsai trees and giving them their name, which means 'plant' (*sai*) 'in a low pot' (*bon*).

It is generally trees or shrubs that are made into bonsai. They can be sourced from the wild, where they have battled against the elements and grown dwarfed as a result (not the easiest option for obtaining a bonsai for most people) or you can buy one from a garden centre or specialist bonsai grower. Alternatively, you can grow your own bonsai from cuttings, seeds or by grafting, which is a bit more difficult. Remember, when you plant the seed for bonsai it will not automatically produce a dwarfed tree; that's why it is important to learn the skills to prune and create a bonsai.

The every day needs of a bonsai tree are exactly the same as those planted outdoors: it must never ever be allowed to dry out (this is fatal), it needs good nourishment and a good growing mixture for it to age, it needs air and light, just like any other plant.

Occasionally, you will come across a bonsai tree that is hundreds of years old, with an extortionate price tag. This is because it has been cared for for many years and is very rare. But as with any hobby, I think it is more exciting to nurture your own bonsai tree and be proud of the way you have maintained it, rather than spend thousands of pounds on someone else's work.

However, if you prefer to buy a ready-cultivated bonsai you can find them at garden centres and specialist nurseries. They are usually of excellent quality, but there are a few key things to remember: besides the age and shape of the tree, you need to check if it is healthy; the soil should be damp, and not rock-hard and dry; the leaves should be bright and healthy, without any spots or scorch marks; and the tree should be secure in its pot, which must have a drainage hole.

There is a little secret to keeping bonsai trees: they are not permanent house plants and appreciate a jaunt outside, when the weather permits, for some fresh air and rain.

People think bonsai are high maintenance, but this is so far from the truth. Just spray daily with water to keep them happy and they will thrive. Bonsai trees are a truly beautiful and stylish way to enhance your home.

BONSAI CARE

Pots & Dishes

In a bonsai's composition its container has a purpose similar to that of a picture frame. Traditionally, the pot must complement the tree and not detract from it by being too bold. As your bonsai will be in the same pot for two to three years, you should pick one with great care.

Size & Shape

Bonsai containers come in various shapes, colours and sizes; you can buy anything from miniature bonsai pots to those as tall as 45 cm (18 in). There are many different types for different bonsai; for example, the large shallow dishes are used for groups of miniature landscapes and the tall containers are usually designed for cascading bonsai. For the bonsai beginner, though, a shallow, oval pot works well with most bonsai styles.

The dimensions of the pot are bound by a number of rules. The pot should be half to one-third of the capacity of the upper part of the tree. Traditionally for the shorter, wider style of bonsai, like the *shakan*, the pot's width should be at least two-thirds of the height of the tree. However, for a tall, slender tree like a *sokan*, the pot must be narrower than the spread of the branches. The depth of the pot must be almost equal to the thickness of the trunk (except with the cascade style).

Colour

It is customary for pot colours to be restrained so that the focus is on the tree itself. Shades of brown, dark blue or green are common and the colour should be influenced by the predominant colour of your tree. However, at geo-fleur we are challenging that tradition and using more modern pots. We use brighter colours for flowering trees, but it's nice to stick to a colour scheme and still choose a pot that complements the colouring of the bonsai. The pot may be glazed outside, but traditionally it shouldn't be glazed inside.

Drainage

All bonsai pots must have drainage holes to allow stale water to drain away and air to circulate around the roots. The holes should be covered with a fine piece of gauze so that the soil does not escape out of the bottom. Bonsai tree roots are not particularly absorbant, and so can quickly become oversaturated with water. A drainage plan is essential to keep your bonsai healthy and happy.

Compost

It is important to use bonsai compost for your tree, as it must be able to hold sufficient moisture and at the same time drain away any excess water to prevent root rot. You also need some akadama, which is a naturally occuring mineral that you mix into the bonsai compost.

A bonsai tree needs air and light,
just like any other plant •

• The leaves should be
bright and healthy

• Bonsai tree roots are thirsty but
not particularly absorbant

The bonsai tree should be secure in its pot •

The soil should be damp
but not soggy •

• Bonsai pots
should have
drainage holes

Watering

The seasons can affect your watering system: if it is very hot in summer your bonsai may need watering twice a day; however, in winter it may only require watering only once every few weeks. The amount of water you need to give depends on how dry the soil is: you only need to water it when it is dry, and add just enough water to make the soil damp. It is really important to keep on top of watering your bonsai, because once the soil is dehydrated it is very hard to bring it back.

You should use a small watering can with a rose attached that has very small holes to give a fine spray; a Haws watering can is my favourite to use. In summer, trees should be watered in the early morning or late afternoon to avoid the midday heat.

Feeding

Fertiliser is important for your bonsai; you can use either liquid fertiliser or fertiliser granules. The liquid form works faster, but the nutrients are used up rapidly – in my opinion, the granules are better for bonsai as they work slowly and last for longer.

There is a rule not to give any fertiliser to a newly repotted bonsai for the first month as the fresh potting compost will have enough nutrients in it already. However, after that pe-riod the trees should be fed with a weak liquid fertiliser every 10–12 days in spring and summer. During winter, bonsai should be given little or no fertiliser, but if you feel your bonsai needs it make sure its soil is still a little damp when applying it.

Wiring

Wiring is when you use wire to manipulate the trunk and/or branches of the tree into your desired shape. It is quite a difficult skill to learn and requires practice. Beginners can learn to judge the tension of wiring by practising on an ordinary tree or shrub; if you wire it too tight the wire will cut into the bark, but if it is too loose it will slip off. Remember to consider the tree from all angles when you are deciding on a shape and ensure it looks good no matter your position.

It is ideal to bend your branch before wiring, as it increases the flexibility. Most bonsai should be wired during the winter months, since they take longer to reach a fixed position, and will remain wired for about 12–18 months, so it is a long process.

How to Wire a Tree

To wire a tree, start from the bottom of the trunk by fixing one end of the wire in the soil. You need to wire at a 45-degree angle, if it is any less than this it won't hold the branch.

Pruning

Bonsai trees need training and pruning throughout their life. Don't be afraid to prune your bonsai. It is vital for the growth of the tree, to help keep its shape, to maintain the small size of a naturally large tree, and to give it the appearance of an age and maturity beyond its real one. You can wire a bonsai into certain shapes, but generally only when the bonsai is young. Once the bonsai is about 2 years old, you need to prune it to give it shape. Most pruning is minimal, but it needs to be carried out frequently in order to force the tree to distribute its growth evenly.

Learning how to prune branches, twigs and leaves is essential to the life of your bonsai. To maintain the health of your bonsai you need to prune any dead or diseased leaves, along with enough leaves to maintain the delicate balance between the size of the root ball and the top growth as you do not want a top-heavy tree.

Pruning also preserves the desired shape of your bonsai tree, as well as keeping the leaves small and helping with the production of flower buds.

Your pruning tools should always be sharp and clean, as using dirty, blunt tools can spread disease and attract pests. If you are heavily pruning cuts of branches, paint the wound afterwards with a protective bonsai cut paste. Pruning shouldn't be rushed and should be done with enough time and the right energy – it's best to be calm!

Tools

As with all hobbies, there are many tools to entice you in as a gardener, especially with bonsai – there are some wonderful tools out there on the market, with beautiful Japanese blades. However, as a beginner you do not need all the expensive tools to get started – you can work up to those. A basic set should include pruning shears, concave branch cutters and wire cutters. Do not swamp your bonsai by using huge tools; buy the right size tools for your bonsai.

Branch and twig pruning

Before you start pruning, decide which side is the front of the tree, and what will be the most natural and best shape to prune the tree into. See pages 60–63 for bonsai styles. Remove any dead or diseased wood, together with any branches growing directly to the front if they are on the lower half of the trunk. To prune a branch it is important to make sure the cut is just above a bud that is pointing in the direction that you want to make the branch grow. Try to make the cut slant downwards so that when you water the plant the water will run off the branches and the chance of rot will be considerably lessened.

The rule to follow when pruning branches is to remove any branch opposite the one that you want to keep – and if there are several branches growing at the same level around the tree they

should be pruned to leave just one branch. Any branches that you have left may now be thinned so that they form a spiral, which becomes more dense nearer to the top of the tree – one of the most beautiful features of a bonsai tree!

These rules also apply to pruning twigs, except twigs do not need to be cut to form a spiral.

Leaf cutting (defoliation)

The tree must be healthy and strong, and at least two years old – so do not do this to recently re-potted or pruned trees as they might be too weak to withstand defoliation. Leaf cutting should be carried out at the start of summer before new leaves start to grow and is one of the secrets of bonsai training – it helps to produce fine growth, smaller leaves and a nice autumn colouring. All you have to do is snip off some or all of the tree's leaves at the top of their stalks, so that the leaf has been removed but its stalk is still attached to the tree. The tree then thinks it is autumn and the petioles, which are the leaf stalks, drop and new, finer leaves grow from the buds.

Repotting and root pruning

Bonsai should only be repotted every two to three years, mainly in spring. You should use roughly the same size pot or one very slightly larger to keep the bonsai small. You will also need some gauze, some sterilised gravel or flint chippings, bonsai compost and akadama. It can be a bit daunting to repot your bonsai after you have cared for it for so long but follow these instructions carefully and your bonsai will be fine.

1. Make sure your new pot is clean, then put a small piece of gauze over its drainage holes.
2. Cover the bottom of the pot with a layer of sterilised gravel or flint chippings. Mix together some compost and akadama at a ratio of 2 tablespoons of compost to 1 tablespoon of akadama, then cover the gravel with the mixture.
3. Remove the bonsai from its existing pot by gently knocking the outside of it with the heel of your hand until the roots become loose.
4. Starting at the edges and working inwards, carefully remove the old soil and tease out the roots with your fingers so that they are no longer clumped together. Remove any dead roots using root scissors and trim back the root ball by one to two thirds depending on the age of the tree.
5. Put the tree in the new pot, taking care not to damage the roots, and fill the pot with more soil (up to 2 cm (¾ in) from the rim of the pot). Finish with a finer layer of bonsai soil.
6. Water the bonsai well and protect it from any harsh sunlight for 48 hours. You do not need to fertilise a newly potted bonsai for one month as the new compost contains nutrients already.

BONSAI STYLES

Bonsai styles are classified by the angle at which the trunk stands in the container. The different styles range from upright and formal to cascading or horizontal. You may prefer to cultivate a mixture of styles or have a particular favourite.

In nature, trees grow in all kinds of forms under the influence of the weather – particularly the wind – and their position. For example, a tree which is growing against a rock will first grow diagonally away from the rock to gain some space, and then vertically towards the light. However, domestic bonsai are pruned and wired into specific styles, allowing you to echo the effects of nature in the comfort of your own home.

Chokkan

This is a formal upright style, which is suitable for *Picea* (spruce), *Larix* (larch), *Juniperus* (juniper), *Zelkova serrata* (Japanese zelkova) and *Gingko biloba* (gingko) trees.

When a tree experiences no competition from other trees, is not sited in a strong prevailing wind and has enough food and water available, it will simply grow straight upwards with a conical trunk. It is important not to arrange the branches symmetrically, and the upper branches must be a little shorter and thinner than the branches below it. Branches must grow horizontally from the trunk, but the tree must be in balance with the tree and the pot.

Shakan

This is a slanting style and suitable for virtually all tree varieties. In nature, a strong prevailing wind will produce a tree which leans naturally to one side. This will also happen if your tree is in the shade and tries to grow towards the light. The trunk can either be straight or slightly bent, but should grow at an angle of between 70 to 80 degrees in relation to the pot.

Fukinagashi

Like the *shakan*, a *fukinagashi* bonsai is shaped by a strong wind, but to an even greater degree. Also called the windswept bonsai – like when we go out in the wind and our hair goes everywhere – this style is suitable for nearly all tree varieties.

This is also a good example of how a bonsai can struggle to survive in the wild: the trunk grows to one side as if the wind has been blowing it constantly. The branches grow out on all sides, but then you train the tree so that they only grow on one side.

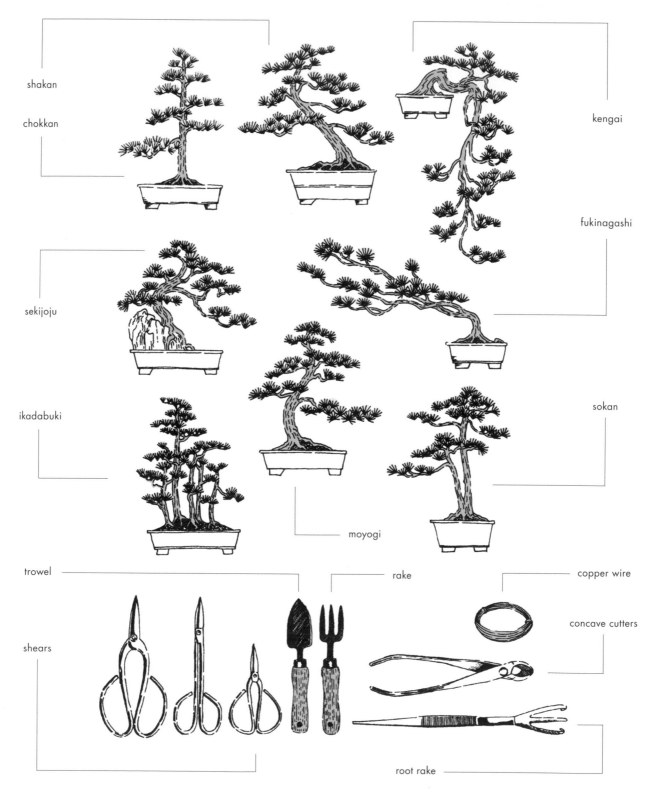

shakan

chokkan

kengai

fukinagashi

sekijoju

ikadabuki

sokan

moyogi

trowel

rake

copper wire

concave cutters

shears

root rake

Moyogi

An informal upright style, the *moyogi* is suitable for nearly all tree varieties. This is one of my favourite styles as it has a number of curves and the lower trunk should be clearly visible. The branches are arranged symmetrically.

Kengai

This is a formal cascade style and one of the most expensive styles of bonsai to buy as it takes a long time to prune. It mimics a tree that has grown on a steep cliff bed and has overhung the cliff face due to its weight or a shortage of light. For bonsai, this means the crown of the tree should be below the rim of the pot. It is quite hard to keep a *kengai* style tree healthy as it is being forced to grow against its natural tendency to grow upwards.

Sekijoju

Trained to grow its roots over a rock, this style emulates rugged, wild trees that survive by sending their roots across rocks in search of nutrients in the hollows. The roots are exposed quickly and look ancient, which is important to this style of bonsai. It is traditional when repotting to ensure that the rock with the roots can be seen as part of the trunk. Good trees for this style are the *Acer* (maple) and *Ulmus parvifolia* (Chinese elm), which have strong roots.

Sokan

A twin trunk style of bonsai that is rather common in nature, where two trunks have grown from a single root, with one trunk thicker than the other. In bonsai, however, this can be faked by propagating a low branch into a second trunk, making sure it's not too high. This style is suitable for all bonsai tree varieties.

Ikadabuki

Also known as the raft style, all varieties of trees can be grown in this shape. It is a good way of grouping lots of trees together, though in nature a fallen tree can survive by throwing up lateral branches, which look like a group of trees. It is important to note the distance between the little trunks is unchanging.

MAKE A MOUNTED STAGHORN FERN PLAQUE

The *Platycerium* is a type of plant commonly known as the staghorn fern because of its striking leaf formations that resemble antlers. Staghorn ferns are also epiphytes, which means they grow by attaching to other plants – usually trees – and get their nutrients from the air, water and collected debris.

This is a fun, plant version of a mounted stag's head; I have used a mount that is usually used in taxidermy for mounting real stag's heads, but you can use a piece of recycled wood if you prefer.

Hang the staghorn fern plaque somewhere prominent in your house, for example, above a fireplace, as a taxidermy stag's head would be mounted. To care for your staghorn fern spray it with water every 3–4 days, ensuring that the moss is kept damp. If you notice that the fern's leaves start to go floppy then it needs more water.

YOU WILL NEED

Platycerium (staghorn fern)

large bowl

carpet moss

water mister (optional)

wooden plaque

moss pins

hammer

1. Remove the staghorn fern from its pot and gently start to brush off the majority of the old soil from its roots using your fingers. It is a good idea to do this over a large bowl, otherwise the soil will get everywhere! Also, be wary of damaging the fern's nucleus, which is the main frilly bit of the plant, as it is very fragile.

2. Lay out the sheet of moss and, if it is quite dry, spray it with a little water to make it easier to manipulate.

3. Decide which side of the staghorn fern you would like to show off. Then, with the best side facing you, lay the roots flat onto the mounting wooden plaque.

4. Wrap the moss all around the staghorn fern's roots and around the edges of the plaque. This can be a little fiddly, so take your time.

5. Once the plant and moss are in the desired position on the plaque, hold the moss down with one hand and gently hammer the moss onto the plaque using the moss pins. Ensure that you do not put the pins directly through the fern's roots and that they are protected by moss. Also, be aware that the moss pins are sharp! They are sometimes hard to get in, but have patience and persevere.

6. Hold up the plaque and check if the fern needs to be secured further, and add more pins as appropriate. You can also add more moss if you would like; spray it with some water first and make sure it is securely held with moss pins.

Tag your #LivingWithPlantsStaghornFern #LivingWithPlantsHowTo @geo_fleur

CACTI

Cacti might seem rather exotic to keep as house plants,
but they make perfect sculptural features and are pretty easy
to maintain. They are also suitable to keep if you own house
pets because their protective spines prevent anyone or
anything getting too close! However, I'd recommend you avoid
buying any sharp-needled cacti if you have young children.

There seems to be a strong divide with cacti: some people find them fascinating while others think they are repulsive. When they spike me or I end up with fine bristles in my fingers for weeks on end, I don't like them either! However, usually I'm in the camp that loves cacti. Not all types of cacti have spines, but they all have bump-like structures called areoles from which the spines or hairy tufts grow. Sometimes these are called bristles and they can feel like felt, but be wary: they are still spiky!

One of the wonderful things about cacti is that they will tolerate terrible behaviour for years and years from you as a plant owner, then they will surprise you with flowers when they get growing again. It is a myth that cacti only flower once in a blue moon: nearly half of all healthy cacti will produce flowers by their third year if cared for correctly. Cacti flower on new growth, which is promoted by caring for them throughout the summer and neglecting them in the winter.

Also, flowering is often stimulated when the plant is pot-bound (where the roots completely fill the pot). Some of the taller candelabra-type cacti and prickly pears need more time to flower, but it is worth the wait – I promise!

The only no-no when it comes to keeping cacti is putting them somewhere damp and cold – they will not survive. Cacti are best kept indoors, and in a heated greenhouse they will thrive. Cacti have been part of the house plant scene for a while, but collections are mostly held by older generations who have collected different varieties and stored them in greenhouses or sun rooms. For people new to keeping house plants this is a great plant group to get started on, as they only require a light misting of water every so often.

There are two types of cacti: forest cacti and desert cacti. Desert cacti are covered in spines, and forest cacti are attached to trees in woodlands and jungles.

Cacti are pretty easy to grow and look after because they need so little water. They love the sun, so are perfect to keep by the window or in a well-lit spot, where they can get plenty of daylight.

TYPES OF CACTI

Desert Cacti

The natural home of desert cacti is the warm semi-desert regions of America. Despite the name of the group, very few can exist in sand alone. Nearly all cacti belong to this group and there are hundreds of varieties to choose from.

To keep your desert cacti thriving, they need to be kept at room temperature from spring to autumn, and in winter no colder than 10°C (50°F). Place them in the sunniest spot in the house. If you keep your cacti in a greenhouse, some shading may be needed in the hottest months.

Use tepid water for your cacti and water more frequently in spring, but less so in winter to prevent shrivelling.

Repotting is best done when a desert cactus is young. Only repot when essential, such as when it is growing out of its pot and needs more room, as they do not like to be disturbed often. See page 113 for tips on how to repot your cacti.

It is easy to take cuttings from cacti (page 132), but let them dry out for a few days before planting them.

Forest Cacti

The typical forest cactus has leaf-like stems and a trailing growth habit. One of my favourites is the *Rhipsalis*, a genus of epiphytic cacti (grows on trees) which produces wonderful flowers when happy. The trick to get a *Rhipsalis* to flower is to provide a cool and dry resting period, and never move the plant once the buds start to appear.

To keep forest cacti really happy, place them where they will experience their ideal temperature of 13–21°C (55–70°F). Keep them in a well-lit spot, but shaded from direct sunlight. Increase watering when their resting period is over, and treat as a normal house plant when flowers appear. During active growth, water liberally when the compost begins to get dry. You should also mist the leaves frequently with water.

It is best to repot forest cacti after flowering has finished. They are easy to propagate – just make sure that you let the cuttings dry out for a few days before inserting them into the potting compost. See page 113 for tips on how to repot your cacti.

SUCCULENTS

Succulents are perfect for lazy indoor gardeners – plus, they look so pretty. They are so easy to maintain and, similar to cacti, come in all shapes and sizes. Succulents are also so Instagrammable – simply dot a few on top of shelves or on a windowsill, and you have a ready-made, picture-perfect snap! They also make the perfect centrepiece when encased in a gorgeous glass terrarium (pages 134–137).

Many people think succulents and cacti are the same thing, as most cacti are classed as succulents. However, although the majority of cacti are also succulents, there are many other succulent plants that are not cacti. The main difference is that cacti always have bumps called areoles from which hair or spikes grow, whereas other kinds of succulents do not. Non-cacti succulents need slightly different growing conditions to cacti; they are a little needier, but still quite easy to care for.

Identifying a succulent is pretty straightforward, as they have thick, fleshy leaves or stems. Many types are a rosette shape and have tightly packed leaves, which help to conserve water in their natural habitat.

Curiously, nearly 40 plant families have at least one succulent member in their group, so it is not surprising that there are hundreds of different succulents to choose from out there. Besides their weird shapes, many succulents have great leaf patterns, colourings and flowers. There has been a huge trend for keeping succulents recently, as they are labelled as low maintenance and they like bright light. You could simply start with an *Echeveria* and *Sempervivum* (houseleek) collection as they can provide an interesting group without any other plants and there are lots of varieties to collect.

Succulents are also great for children to care for as they can withstand a great deal of neglect and are very easy to propagate, which is great fun for kids. Take offsets or leaf cuttings (page 132) and let them dry out for a couple of days before planting in compost. Water very sparingly and do not cover.

How to keep
your succulents happy

————

Keep succulents at room temperature; in winter around 10–13°C (50–55°F) is ideal. They like bright windowsills, especially if they are south-facing, but would appreciate some shade when it is really hot. This makes them perfect bathroom plants. From spring to autumn, water the plants from the bottom and do not water them again until the compost begins to really dry out. In the winter, practically neglect them and water only every one to two months. Overwatering is a big killer for succulents – they don't actually require that much. Misting the leaves is a great way to water succulents, then give them a good drink from the bottom once every two weeks if they look particularly dry.

Repot when the succulent is growing literally out of its pot, and transfer to a slightly larger one.

MAKE A KOKEDAMA

A kokedama is a Japanese hanging moss ball. Instead of potting the plant, the roots are encased in a ball of moss, then the whole creation is suspended from strings. Plants that work well in a kokedama include the *Nephrolepis exaltata* (Boston fern) and *Adiantum* (maidenhair fern).

I sometimes hang my kokedama from a picture hook, but it also looks good hanging from a curtain rail. Ferns like humidity, so a perfect location for your kokedama is a bathroom or a sunny conservatory. To water your kokedama, submerge the moss ball in a bowl or sink of water, plant side up – do not let the stem of the plant go into the water, you just want the moss ball to be submerged. Allow it to soak up the water for 10–20 minutes or until it is fully saturated. Remove the kokedama from the water and gently squeeze the moss ball to get rid of the excess water. Ready to make one?

YOU WILL NEED

[1 scoop = approx. 20 g/7 oz]

1 scoop of akadama

2 scoops of John Innes soil

2 scoops of Irish peat moss

large bowl

fern such as *Adiantum* (maidenhead fern)

approx. 30 × 30 cm (12 × 12 in) square
    sheet of carpet moss

twine or metal wire

1. Put 1 scoop of akadama, 2 scoops of John Innes soil and 2 scoops of Irish peat moss into the bowl; if you want to mix more to make a bigger kokedama or more than one, just keep the ratio of the 3 different growing mediums the same. Mix everything together until the mixture is evenly combined.

2. Mix in a touch of water, making sure everything is well blended. Gradually add a little more water, thoroughly mixing it in after each addition, until the mixture sticks together and drips slightly – do not add too much water at once as it is difficult to remove excess water.

3. Take the fern out of its pot and gently shake off the soil, or tease it away with your fingers, until the majority of the roots are exposed. It can feel like you are damaging the plant at this point, but don't worry – you are not hurting it.

4. Using your hands, cover the roots with the wet soil mixture until there is a 2 cm- (¾ in-) thick layer all the way around; form it into a ball about the same volume as the plant's original pot. Give the ball a squeeze to release the water.

5. Lay out a blanket of sheet moss to envelop the ball and put the ball in the centre. Gather the moss around the plant to make sure all the mixture is covered; the moss needs to be securely wrapped around the ball but not so tightly that you compact the growing medium and squash the plant's roots.

6. Wrap the twine around the moss ball to keep it in place by starting at the top of the root ball and wrapping around at an angle to make sure it is all bound together and secure. Finish by wrapping the twine around the top of the ball a couple of times and then tie the two ends together – be careful not to tie around the stem of the plant and only around the moss. Make a double knot so it is nice and secure.

7. Finally, cut a separate length of twine to create a loop of your desired length. Tie the ends to the twine wrapped round the moss, with one end tied to either side of the ball. You're now ready to hang your kokedama with pride!

Tag your finished #LivingWithPlantsHowTo #LivingWithPlantsKokedama @geo_fleur

FERNS

Ferns are quite easy to maintain when you know how. They can be considered to be quite needy plants, but if cared for properly, they will reward you with lush green fronds all year round. *Asplenium nidus* or bird's nest fern (pictured opposite) is a great indoor plant and looks quite different to other ferns. Moisture is very important for them to thrive and grow well. The attractive, spear-like fronds should look shiny when the plant is in good health.

Ferns were extremely popular during the Victorian era and large collections were grown in conservatories, in terrariums or glass cases. Their popularity waned because they were easily damaged by coal fires, but when central heating came along ferns came back into favour.

Most ferns are not difficult to grow, but they will not tolerate neglect; if you go on holiday for a fortnight and forget about them, they will not be happy. Their compost must never be allowed to dry out and the surrounding air needs to be kept moist. They love being in bathrooms – if you keep them elsewhere, mist with water regularly.

Many ferns are formed of a rosette of divided arching leaves called fronds, which unfold into a beautiful performance of foliage. These fronds are delicate and need room to develop, so when putting a fern next to the rest of your plant gang make sure they have space to grow. If any fronds die off, make sure you remove them so new ones can grow.

My favourite ferns are the *Nephrolepis exaltata* (Boston fern) and *Asparagus setaceus* (asparagus fern). The *Adiantum* (maidenhair fern) comes in at a sly third – however, it is not as forgiving as other ferns if you forget to water it as its leaves go very crispy very quickly.

How to keep your ferns happy

Keep ferns nice and warm, at around 16–21°C (60–70°F) . Most people think that ferns are shade lovers, but that is not true. They love indirect light; an east- or north-facing windowsill is ideal. Ferns also love to be kept moist, so make sure you give them a regular misting. Water them from the bottom and never let the soil dry out – this does not mean you should keep the soil soggy, as waterlogging will lead to rotting; just keep the soil moist. Do not water them as much in winter as they do not drink as much water in the colder months. Most ferns are fast-growing and will need repotting (pages 108–113) annually, but be careful not to bury any part of the fern's stems or leaves as this could cause the plant to rot.

above left: *The* Adiantum *(maidenhair fern) needs
constant moisture, so can be a little tricky to grow;
but this makes it perfect to use in terrariums.*
above right: *The* Asparagus setaceus *(Asparagus fern)
is one of the easiest ferns to grow (although it still
won't tolerate neglect!). The luscious arching fronds
make it ideal for hanging in baskets.*

BROMELIADS & AIR PLANTS

Many of the house plants that we have in our homes
are from tropical lands, but none are as exotic as the
Bromeliaceae (bromeliads). *Bromeliaceae* are a large family
of plants that includes the genus *Tillandsia*, which are
commonly called air plants.

Bromeliads

When people refer to bromeliads they usually mean the species that have rosettes of leaves, which produce spectacularly coloured bracts – modified leaves that look like petals. The rosettes form a vase-like vessel for catching rainwater in their native tropical American homes.

Bromeliads are easy to grow, but the key is to water down the vase of the plant where the flower-like bracts grow, to simulate rainwater. Many bromeliads are epiphytes, which are plants that attach themselves to another plant for structure. Epiphytes thrive on the nutrients in the air, water and from whatever debris falls into their vase – the roots are just to hold them in place.

They like to be kept nice and warm at around 21°C (70°F), so do not let them get too cold; 10°C (50°F) is about as low as they will tolerate.

Air plants

The *Tillandsia* (air plant), which was popular in the 70s, has become cool again; like fashion, plant and gardening styles come and go. Lots of bloggers and interior designers are using them in weird and wonderful displays. Small shops selling home items and ceramics are starting to stock them too, though they will not have the same knowledge as a specialist garden centre or nursery. You can also buy air plants on the internet and they survive shipping well,

but if possible it is better to pick out your air plant in person so that you can check the health of the plant beforehand.

It is important to do some research into which variety of air plant would be best for you before you buy one. Pick one that suits your own taste with regards to its texture, shape and colour. It is so tempting to buy an air plant when it is blooming or about to flower, but since the flower is not a permanent fixture make sure you are content with the plant's overall shape and form.

Be careful not to buy a *Tillandsia* that is shrivelled or looks brown, as it might be close to dying. However, brown, decaying leaves at the base of the *Tillandsia* are normal and need not be a deterrent.

Watering air plants

Air plants are like sponges: if you regularly mist a sponge it will stay moist; however, if you let a sponge dry out completely you will have to totally soak it to make it moist again. An air plant is the same – this means that it is extra important to water them correctly. This makes the bathroom an ideal spot for airplants.

There are many different ways to water *Tillandsias* and it is easy to get confused about which method works best for each type of air plant. There is also the myth that air plants do not need to be watered at all, which is incorrect as all plants need air and water to photosynthesise. There are three ways you can water air plants: misting, soaking and dunking. When soaking or dunking your air plants, always remember to leave them to dry out before watering again, as otherwise they can suffer from rot.

1. Misting is great for air plants in a container or display that you cannot remove the plants from, but you need to remember to mist daily. If this is the plant's only source of water you need to saturate the plant with the misting. Be careful not to get water all over your furniture and electrical appliances!

2. Some air plants such as the *Tillandsia xerographica* appreciate a good dunk in a bowl of water for a few minutes.

3. You can also soak air plants in a bowl of water for 1 hour, deep enough to submerge the plant completely. It satisfies their thirst a little longer and you only need to do this once a week.

Combine different shapes, textures and sizes of plants to create a plant gang. Mix up plastic and terracotta pots, too!

MAKE A TRIANGLE XEROGRAPHICA HOLDER

Xerographica is a wonderful plant on its own, but it's somewhat magical when it's hung or displayed in a shape or holder. This brass holder is a beautifully chic way to show off your air plants.

I like to pop it on a surface like a shelf; however, you could hang it with fishing line and suspend it against a window or in a doorway. You can get copper and brass piping from most hardware stores, along with the other tools needed to make this.

YOU WILL NEED
ruler
1.08 m (3 ft 6 in) of 3 cm (1¼ in)
    diameter copper or brass piping
hacksaw
wire cutters
spool of 1 mm-thick copper wire
Tillandsia xerographica

1. Measure out 3 × 10 cm (4 in) pieces of piping and 3 × 13 cm (5 in) pieces of piping, then cut them off using the hacksaw.

2. Use the wire cutters to cut a long piece of copper wire about 2 m (6 ft 7 in) long.

3. Thread the shorter pieces of piping onto the copper wire, leaving about 1.5 m (5 ft) of loose wire at one end of the row of piping. Be careful, as both the wire and the edges of the piping are sharp.

4. Fold the pipes at the joints into a triangle and wrap over the wire at the join to keep the triangle in place. This is the base triangle of the holder.

5. Thread 2 of the longer pieces of piping onto the long length of wire. Fold the pipes over at their joint to make another triangle and secure the wire at the joint where the longer pipe meets the shorter pipe.

6. Thread the longer piece of wire that you have just been working with through the shorter base pipe towards the joint that currently does not have a third pipe coming off it.

7. Thread the last piece of piping onto the same piece of wire. Wrap the wire over the top joint several times to make sure that all the pieces are secure and will not slip off the wire.

8. Cut off the excess wire at both corners and tuck the ends into a piece of piping to hide them. Hang your *Tillandsia xerographica* wherever you like!

Tag your finished #LivingWithPlantsPlantHolder #LivingWithPlantsHowTo @geo_fleur

CHAPTER THREE

TOOLS, MATERIALS & BASIC TECHNIQUES

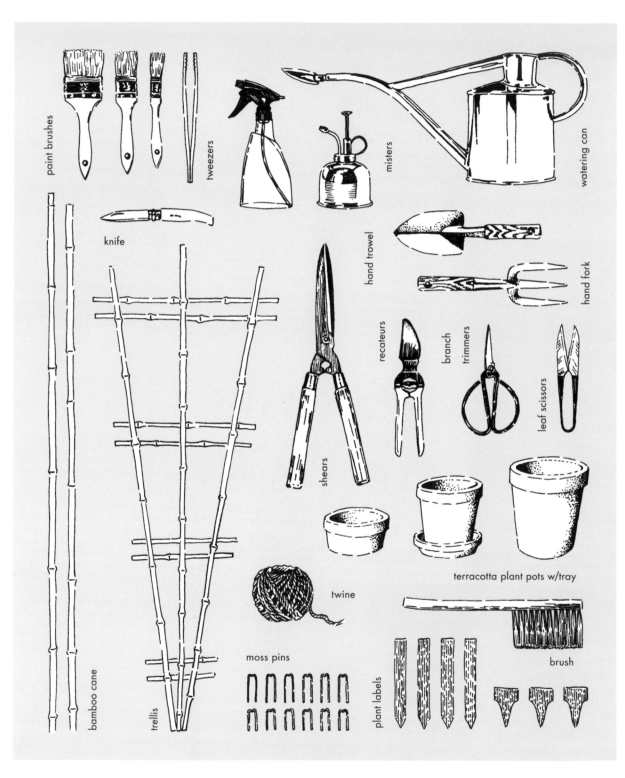

paint brushes

tweezers

knife

misters

watering can

hand trowel

hand fork

recateurs

branch trimmers

leaf scissors

shears

terracotta plant pots w/tray

bamboo cane

trellis

twine

moss pins

plant labels

brush

TOOLS

As with many hobbies, you can find a vast array of tools for keeping plants. Some are super expensive, which you can dream about buying for when you have your urban jungle. I first began my plant gang with just a few key tools, which is everything you need to get started.

Essential items

To begin gardening indoors, you'll need a collection of pots and containers in which to grow your plants. Simple plastic or terracotta pots are essential. There is also a lovely range of different ceramic pots out on the market, but check that they have drainage holes, especially if you are growing ferns or plants that need lots of moisture.

Pots are measured across the top, inside the rim, and the diameter is given either in centimetres or inches. I find the most useful sizes are generally 6.5 cm (2½ in), 9 cm (3½ in), 12 cm (4¾ in) and 18 cm (7 in). You may also need a few larger pots for mature plants.

You will also need saucers or trays to stand the pots in, so you can water your plants from the bottom and stop pots from dripping all over your beautiful furniture. You can put a pot with drainage holes inside another decorative container that does not have holes to catch water, but make sure you always check that the plant is not left standing in water. Whether you have watered the plant from the top or bottom, lift the inner pot out after an hour and discard any water still left in the bottom. Leaving a plant stood in water for long periods of time is an easy and common way to kill it – you willl cause the roots to rot. If in doubt, it's better to underwater your plants! Finally, you need a mister to spritz your plants, which is great to increase humidity.

Once you start to get a collection of plants going, there are a few more tools that are needed for maintaining them. Specific tools are required for the How To projects, but here is a general tool list to begin your journey.

Watering can with a long spout and fine nozzle: I love Haws watering cans as they do some great colours and sizes of this classic style – my favourite is the copper. Haws also make beautiful plant misters, which come in a brass or silver. You can, of course, use a plastic plant sprayer to mist your plants, which are also used for spraying plants with fertiliser or pest control – but please do not confuse the two or you will end up with some sad plants!

Plant scissors or long-handled scissors: Really useful for deadheading or trimming back and pruning.

Root clippers: A great tool for repotting or propagating plants.

Small brushes, such as paint brushes: Handy for brushing stray soil or gravel off plants.

Bamboo sticks and trellis: Ideal for providing plants support and to train them into specific spaces.

Floristry mossing pins: Fantastic for holding down mosses and fixing pieces of moss together.

Ball of string or garden twine: Useful to secure plants that get a little out of control.

Plant labels: For remembering and identifying plant varieties and dates planted.

Chopsticks or tweezers: Essential for handling any cacti.

POTTING COMPOSTS

Using the right kind of growing medium for your plants is very
important, as different plants need different nutrients. Please
do not use a soil or compost that is not right for your plant;
this can be detrimental to the plant and even cause it to die.

Unfortunately, you cannot just use ordinary garden soil for house plants as it contains weed seeds and could have pests and diseases in it, which are not things you want to bring into your home! Instead, you should use a purpose-made potting compost (also called potting mix in the US).

There are two main types of potting compost: soil-based and soilless. Grit or sand can be added to both to improve the drainage. There are also specialist growing mediums made for specific types of plant. For example, most bromeliads are epiphytic, which means they grow by attaching themselves to other plants, usually trees, and cannot be grown in normal soil. They get their nutrients from rotting vegetable matter and bark that accumulates in the crevices of trees, and so need a special bromeliad compost. Cacti and succulents also need a purpose-made cactus potting compost, which is very free-draining.

Up until about 1940 many different potting mixtures were used, as gardeners had to make their own composts with no scientific guidance. These often contained ingredients of varying quality and unhygienic animal manures. Results were consequently unreliable and plant diseases were a common problem.

In an attempt to standardise and reduce the number of different potting mixtures growers needed, two researchers at the John Innes Horticultural Institute in Britain developed a set of formulae to make four types of compost suited for the different stages in a plant's development: John Innes seed compost for sowing seeds and striking cuttings (pages 132–133); John Innes No.1 for young seedlings and rooted cuttings; John Innes No.2 for general potting and ideal for most medium-size plants; and John Innes No.3 for larger and/or more mature plants. The formulae for these mixtures were published in 1939 and today are the standard for most UK commercial composts, which are also sterilised to eliminate pest and diseases.

Several universities in the US, as well as a number of commercial firms, also did research into the best compositions for compost, but the US does not have an equivalent standardised system.

For US growers, it is worth researching the different potting mixes available to you and choosing a good-quality mixture appropriate to the stage of potting and type of plant. Alternatively, you can make your own John Innes mixtures by following their formulae, which are easily found online. Generally speaking though, many multipurpose, house plant or loam-based composts will be suitable for most indoor house plants. If in doubt, just ask at your local garden centre or do some research on-line first.

Soil-based composts

The soil in soil-based composts is traditionally loam, which is a type of naturally occurring soil composed of sand, clay and humus (decomposed matter, not the chickpea dip!). Loam is rich in nutrients and retains moisture while also having good drainage. Some soil-based composts are no longer made of loam, but these are not as good so it is best to use a loam-based one. The loam is broken down into a finer mixture and sterilised

to get rid of any nasties. These composts are made to hold moisture and have added fertilisers, and are ideal for holding plants firmly in place. When using soil-based compost, make sure that you press the soil down into the pot so that it is well compacted.

Soilless composts

Soilless potting composts are traditionally made from peat, which is a very soft, naturally occurring nutrient- and moisture-rich growing medium. Peat is taken from peatlands, which are stable ecosystems that contain specialised plants and take thousands of years to develop. Because of this, using peat is very bad for the environment, so it is preferable to use a peat-substitute compost, which does not cause damage. Both peat-based and peat-substitute composts tend to dry out rather easily and are difficult to rehydrate once they do. Unlike soil-based compost, you must be careful not to compact soilless compost as it will suffer from lack of air.

PLANT HERBS
IN VINTAGE TINS

At geo-fleur we love to plant herbs in vintage-inspired tins, which you can buy online, but you can use tins with any designs you fancy. You need to use small plastic pots of herbs for this How To, so that they fit inside the tins. Plant a selection of different herbs of your choice – my favourites are basil, rosemary and thyme – and remember that plants tend to look better grouped in odd numbers. I think five or seven look perfect for a kitchen windowsill.

To care for your herbs, make sure the topsoil is moist and if they become dry, mist them with water. Do not pour water into the tins as they do not have any drainage holes and too much water will make the herbs rot.

a variety of different herbs

vintage-inspired tins

multipurpose compost

1. Take the herbs out of their plastic pots. If you buy them from a supermarket they are often pot-bound – where the roots fill the pot and start to grow through the drainage holes – so be wary of this when pulling them out of their plastic pot. If it is tough to get the plant out of the pot, tickle the bottom of the roots coming through the pot and the plant should come loose.

2. Gently remove the majority of the soil from around the plant's roots with your fingers.

3. Add enough multipurpose compost into the bottom of the tin for the top of the plant's roots to sit about 2 cm (¾ in) below the top of the tin.

Put the herb into the tin, then add some more compost around (if there is space) and on the top of the plant's roots. Press down to make sure it is secure in the tin, but do not press too hard as you do not want to compact the compost too much and squash the roots.

4. Repeat steps 1–3 until you have planted up all your herbs. Arrange them on a windowsill ready to use in your cooking and add a gorgeous vintage touch to your kitchen.

Tag your finished #LivingWithPlantsTins #LivingWithPlantsHowTo @geo_fleur

POTTING

There will be times when you need to repot your plants,
whether they have been in the same pot for so long that their
growing medium has become depleted or they have outgrown
their original pot, known as potting on.

Knowing how to repot your plants is one of the most important skills for the indoor gardener to learn. Almost any plant can be grown in a pot with the right potting mixture. But always make sure you use fresh potting compost, not old compost that has already been used for another plant or soil from the garden; neither of these will have enough nutrients in them for repotting a plant.

Nowadays, potting mixture has been formulated specifically for use in pots. It holds moisture without becoming waterlogged as it allows excess water to drain out. It also contains the right amount of fresh nutrients, which is why it is important to use new compost. Depending on their size and how established they are, many house plants like to grow in multipurpose, house

plant or loam-based compost; however, some plants like orchids and cacti are not suited to any of the general-purpose potting mixtures.

As I mentioned earlier, there are certain plant pots that promote healthy growth, and now there is a movement toward self-watering pots. At geo-fleur we use Bosske self-watering containers they make cool sky planters that hang upside-down from the ceiling. These are great for hanging displays as you only need to top up the water reservoir every two weeks or so, rather than climbing up a ladder every day. They are also perfect for busy or forgetful plant owners!

When you are just getting started with your urban jungle collection, it is a good idea to grow your plants in plastic pots with drip trays underneath, as they need watering less frequently than

The Pilea peperomiodies is also called a Missionary Plant or Pancake Plant. Pilea is one of the easiest plants to propogate. See pages 132–133 to learn more about propagation.

those in clay pots – it is vital to remember this, as overwatering is a major killer of pot plants. Clay and ceramic pots are great to pot into once your plants are more established and are settled into their environment. Of course, these are more expensive, so once you have decided on the one you want it is worth buying it a size up. However, this only applies if you have a slow-growing plant; something like a fast-growing *Monstera deliciosa* (Swiss cheese plant) will need potting up fairly regularly if you buy it as a small plant.

Repotting

Repotting is the process of taking a well-established plant out of its current pot and putting it in a new pot of the same size, containing fresh potting compost. This is best done when a plant is at rest, usually in spring. For plants that bloom in winter, it's best to repot them in autumn, just after their dormant period. Follow these simple instructions when repotting your plants:

1. Take the plant out of its existing pot by gently squeezing the sides and holding on to the roots.

2. Remove some of the old soil by carefully rubbing and massaging the plant's roots. Lay the plant down while you prepare the new pot.

3. Clean out the old pot or use a clean new pot the same size as the old one. You can cover the drainage holes with some broken pot or stones, which is sometimes called crocking, before adding the fresh potting mixture. This is not so essential with plastic plant pots, which usually have lots of holes in the bottom, but it is a good idea and helps with drainage.

4. Add suitable fresh potting mixture on top of the crocking (if using) and pop the plant inside the pot; make sure it is standing straight and in the centre of the pot, and the top of the root ball is about 2.5 cm (1 in) from the top of the pot. Remove or add some potting mixture from under the plant to get it to the required height.

5. Hold the plant in place with one hand while putting more potting mixture around the sides of the plant. Make sure that your plant remains straight and centred, and fill with potting mixture to just cover the top of the roots. The space at the top of the pot gives space for watering.

6. Gently press down the new potting mix with sufficient pressure to hold the plant securely, but do not press too hard as this can hinder drainage.

Potting on

When you begin growing your collection in pots, never use an unnecessarily large pot. Start your plant off in the smallest possible pot and move it on to a larger one as its roots fill the current one; this technique is called potting on. It ensures that the plant regularly gets fresh compost and nutrients for its roots to grow through.

Generally you should only pot on a plant when it has become pot-bound (when a plant seems to have stopped growing). The way to tell if a plant is pot-bound is to look at the drainage holes at the bottom of the pot. The roots will be matted and coiled around to such an extent that no potting mixture will be visible – the roots may have even started growing out through the surface of the soil.

When potting on, choose a pot about 4 cm (1½ in) larger in diameter to allow extra space for the roots. Ensure your new container is clean then follow the instructions for repotting, remembering to repot into your bigger pot (pages 112–113).

REPOTTING YOUR PLANTS

Here are some useful tips to help you when repotting your plants. It can seem like quite a tricky process at first, but you'll soon get the hang of it! It's really important you are able to master repotting, as it will really help your plant to flourish and thrive.

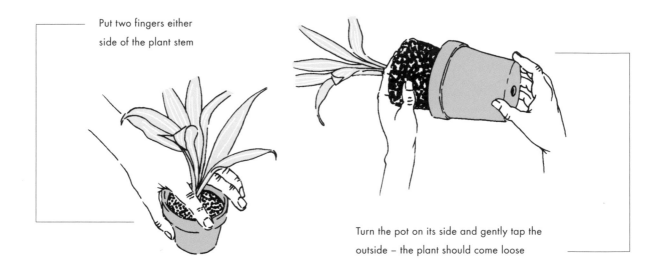

Put two fingers either side of the plant stem

Turn the pot on its side and gently tap the outside – the plant should come loose

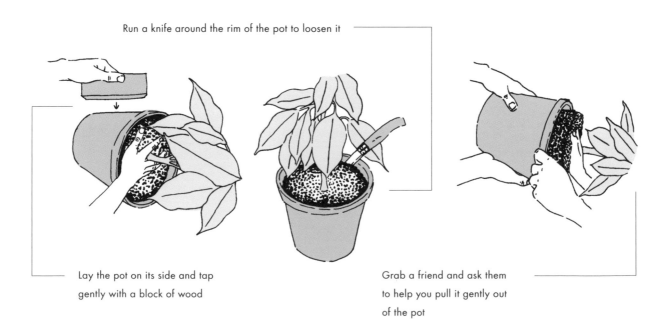

Run a knife around the rim of the pot to loosen it

Lay the pot on its side and tap gently with a block of wood

Grab a friend and ask them to help you pull it gently out of the pot

POT-BOUND REPOTTING (POTTING ON)

Take the plant out of the pot – if the roots are very close to the edge of the pot and coiled, this is a sign of being pot-bound

Repot into a bigger pot, about 4 cm (1½ in) larger in diameter

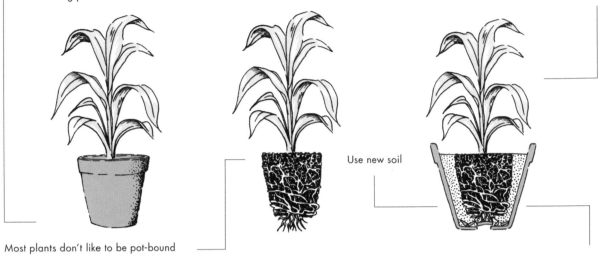

Use new soil

Most plants don't like to be pot-bound

Put crocks (broken terracotta) or large stones in the bottom to help with drainage

REPOTTING CACTI

Repotting a cactus can be tricky (and painful!). A cactus should be repotted as soon as the roots begin to show through the drainage holes at the bottom of the pot.

Push a pencil through the base to unhook the roots

Hold the cactus in its new pot and add even amounts of soil all around to make sure that it is nice and steady in its new home

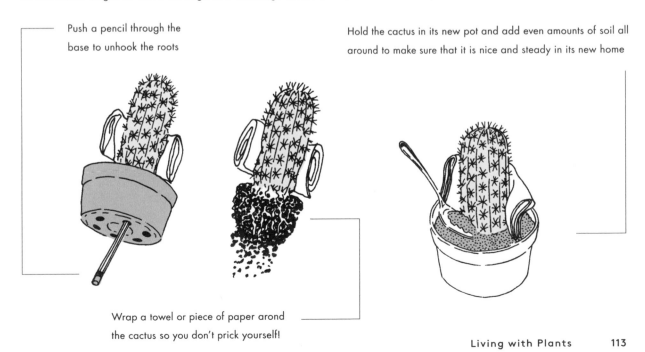

Wrap a towel or piece of paper arond the cactus so you don't prick yourself!

GROWING PLANTS IN A TERRARIUM

Bring the beauty of an outdoor garden indoors, with a stunning glass terrarium. There are a few rules to follow when making a terrarium: from soil and plant type to which container to choose from.

See How To Make a Closed Terrarium on pages 116–119 and How To Make an Open Terrarium on pages 134–137 to learn how to make your own miniature gardens. Terrariums are a gorgeous way of bringing nature inside, especially if you don't have a garden or an outside space. But what exactly is a terrarium? A terrarium is a glass container that either partially or completely encloses the plants that are growing inside it. If the terrarium has a permanent opening it is an open terrarium, but if the opening is sealed once the plants are inside it is a closed terrarium. There are also many different varieties of terrariums, including desert, forest and aquatic.

Terrarium gardening is low-maintenance and super easy, but the end result is always stunning. They are perfect for first time indoor gardeners and make wonderful gifts. It is important that you keep compatible plants together, as they will have the same growing patterns and will require similar attention. For example, desert plants like cacti and succulents are best grouped together in an open terrarium (pages 134–137) as they require adequate air circulation, whereas tropical plants like ferns and nerve plants suit an enclosed terarrium (pages 116–119) as they need a warm and humid environment to thrive.

So what's the appeal of these contained miniature gardens? They are magnificent living sculptures and can be enjoyed all year round. They also make show-stopping centrepieces and are a classy way to add a touch of green to any room. But most importantly, a terrarium can look good in any space, big or small!

MAKE A CLOSED TERRARIUM

Closed terrariums differ to open terrariums in that their vessels are designed to be sealed shut after they have been planted up. Once sealed, the terrarium creates its own ecosystem, recycling air, nutrients and water entirely inside the container. This means that you may never need to open your terrarium again.

This How To uses *Pteridophytes* (ferns) and *Fittonia* (nerve plants) as they like the humidity of a closed terrarium, but other plants you can use are *Hypoestes phyllostachya* (polka dot plants), *Adiantum* (maidenhead fern) and *Nephrolepsis exaltata* (Boston fern). I like to use different coloured nerve plants to balance out the green ferns.

metal teaspoon

soft fine artist's paint brush

long metal skewers

tape

piece of paper, or a kitchen funnel

glass demijohn and cork bung, or other
   clear glass vessel with an airtight lid

multipurpose compost

activated charcoal

small natural stones

2–3 different coloured *Fittonia* (nerve plants)

1–2 *Pteridophytes* (ferns)

thin kitchen tongs

moss

1. Make a long-handled spoon and long-handled paint brush by securely attaching each one to a skewer with tape.

2. Make a funnel out of a piece of paper, or use a kitchen funnel if you have one, and place it into the opening of the vessel. Carefully spoon the compost into the funnel, allowing the compost to drop to the bottom of the terrarium before spooning in more. For the size of terrarium we are making here, the soil needs to be about 5–6 cm (2–2½ in) deep.

3. Add 3 tablespoons of activated charcoal on top of the compost and give it a little stir using your long-handled spoon – don't be too vigorous as you do not want to splash the mixture up the sides of the jar. Drop in a few stones.

4. Carefully remove one of the plants from its pot; if it is pot-bound (where the roots have started to grow out the bottom of the pot) and difficult to remove, tap the bottom of the pot and the plant should release. Hold the plant over a bowl and use your fingers to take off the majority of the old soil, which you can discard.

5. Pick up the plant with the tongs, or use two long skewers or chopsticks if you do not have any thin tongs. Squeeze the plant through the neck of the demijohn or vessel opening and lower it into the position you want. Do not worry about damaging the plant as it will only be squashed for a moment while you get it inside the container.

6. Repeat steps 4 and 5 with the remaining plants, making sure that the soil is secure and compact around the plants.

7. Once all the plants are in situ, you can add some decorative topping. Here, we added some moss and small natural stones. Lower them into the terrarium as you did with the greenery and place them around the plants.

8. If any of the plants have soil or other bits on their leaves, use the paint brush to gently dust the debris off. Seal the terrarium using a cork bung or the vessel's airtight lid. Display with pride.

Tag your finished #LivingWithPlantsTerrarium #LivingWithPlantsHowTo @geo_fleur

CHAPTER FOUR

PLANT CARE

ENVIRONMENT

Choosing the right place in your home to keep a particular
plant is crucial to its wellbeing and even its survival. Different
types of plants have different needs when it comes to light,
temperature and humidity, so it is important you find your
plants a spot that meets their requirements.

While you may have your heart set on keeping certain plants in a specific space, if the environment is not right for the plant there is no point trying to make it grow there. Forcing a plant into the wrong space will only lead to trouble. It is much better to first work out the light levels, temperature and air quality in a room, and then choose plants that like those conditions. There is such a huge variety of house plants out there that you will definitely be able to find some that are perfect for you and your space.

Light

When you see a plant you want to buy, before purchasing, think about where it is going to live once you get it home – you do not want a sun-loving plant to be left in a shady corner, for example. See page 47 for guidance on how the direction in which a room's window faces affects the light in that space.

Any good garden centre will advise you on what a particular plant likes, but make sure you read the plant labels and follow the notes for each plant as different varieties of the same type of plant can desire different levels of light.

Most house plants prefer bright, filtered and natural light, but there are lots that like plenty of shade too. However, all plants need at least some light in order to photosynthesise (use light to convert carbon dioxide and water into sugars) and grow. If a plant does not get enough light it will grow long, weak stems as it strains to search for more light. On the other hand, if a plant gets more light than it can withstand, its leaves will shrivel up and fall off, or become very pale. The compost will also get dry very quickly, so be wary. Whichever plants you choose, with the exception of desert cacti, do not let them bake on a windowsill in the boiling midday sun – it is not fair!

Because plants use their leaves to absorb light, cleaning the leaves not only makes the plant look pretty, but also helps the plant thrive. Misting plants helps to keep their leaves clean, or you can buy leaf cleaning products called leaf shine that can be used on plants with smooth, glossy leaves – just avoid using it on hairy or spiky plants.

OTHER WAYS TO INCREASE HUMIDITY

Sit plants in damp gravel, which will help the plants trap moisture between their leaves

Sit the plant on a wooden block in a saucer filled with water to keep the soil damp

Place the plant pot within a second, larger pot and fill with moss to increase moisture levels

Mist with filtered water

Temperature

Different plants like different levels of heat, so always check the plant's label to find out how warm or cool it likes to be kept. Just as you should consider the amount of light a particular room gets, you should also take into account how hot or cold the space is – plants that like cool environments will not survive if you live in a sauna and those that need plenty of warmth will not live in a cold, dark corner.

Air and humidity

During the day, plants perform a process known as photosynthesis in which they convert carbon dioxide and water into sugars. Plants produce oxygen as a byproduct of this process. However, at night, photosynthesis stops and a process called respiration occurs, in which plants take up oxygen and produce carbon dioxide. Consequently, it is important for plants to be provided with the correct airflow.

Opening a window to provide some ventilation helps to keep plants cool when it is hot, but do not let them sit in a draft. Some house plants will shed their leaves and wilt if they are exposed to cold currents of air, but gentle air movement helps to reduce the likelihood of fungal diseases, so it is better not to have plants shut in a room with no ventilation.

Desert cacti and succulents love dry air, but most house plants prefer air that is moist – many plants wilt when the central heating is on because it dries out the air. If you need to increase the humidity of the air around a plant you can create a microclimate for it by creating wet gravel trays to go underneath your house plants. Misting your plants helps to increase the humidity and freshen up the foliage (see diagrams above).

WATERING & FEEDING

The top killer for indoor plants is overwatering: don't do it!

Many people think that they are being kind to their plants by giving them plenty of water, but instead overwatering will cause plants to rot. Some plants will need watering daily, but others just once a month. This is why it is important to pay attention to a plant's care instructions. You should also be aware of the type of pot you are using, as you will often find that plants in terracotta or clay pots need more frequent watering than those in plastic pots because they allow more water to evaporate.

One of the skills that you need to learn to properly look after your house plant collection is to judge when your plants need watering by checking whether the compost is too wet or too dry.

Never leave your plants for so long without water that the leaves begin to droop; some plants cannot come back from this stage, so do not let them get that bad. There are fancy water meters on the market that measure a plant's water levels, but it is an easy skill to learn – just pay close attention to how your plants' leaves and compost look until you become well-practiced at spotting the early signs that your plants need watering.

Some plants do not like hard tap water; ideally, you should use rainwater or filtered tap water. When watering your plant, give it enough water so that it reaches all the parts of the pot, but do not flood the plants, as the nutrients in the compost will be washed away. It is really important not to leave plant pots sitting in water as this encourages the plants to rot – check an hour after watering and if there is still water in the bottom of the decorative pot the inner pot is sat in, or in the saucer the pot is stood on, then tip it away. See the illustrations opposite to see how to water plentifully, moderately and sparingly.

Different ways to water your plant

There are a number of different ways of watering your plants and the method you use depends on the type of plant – some plants prefer a 'little and often' approach, whereas others like a good drenching but only every now and again.

Top watering (fig.1, page 126)
Water the plant at the top of its pot using a long-spouted watering can to apply the water to the compost – try to avoid watering the leaves.

Bottom watering (fig.2, page 126)
This is my fail-safe trick to revive unhappy plants. Pop a saucer filled with water under the pot; the plant can then absorb as much water as it needs without any danger of overwatering. Once it has taken up what it wants, remove the plant and put it back in its usual decorative pot or tray.

HOW TO WATER PLENTIFULLY

1. Do the soil finger test: press your finger into the soil. If it's damp, the plant does not need watering yet

2. Water from both top and bottom

3. Tip away any excess water after 1 hour

HOW TO WATER MODERATELY

3. Tip away any excess water

2. Water from the top only

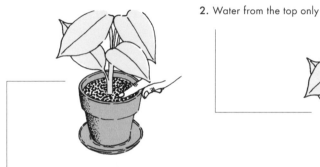

1. Do the soil finger test: press your finger into the soil. If it's damp, the plant does not need watering yet

HOW TO WATER SPARINGLY

2. Water from the top

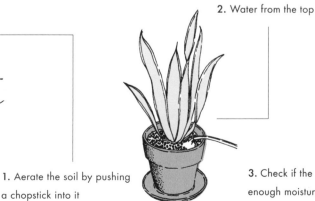

1. Aerate the soil by pushing a chopstick into it

3. Check if the plant has had a chance to soak up enough moisture, but never leave it sitting in water

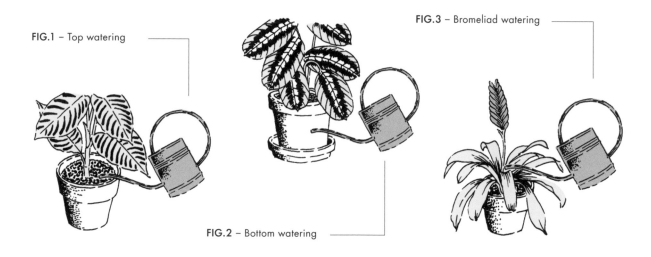

FIG.1 – Top watering

FIG.2 – Bottom watering

FIG.3 – Bromeliad watering

If the plant pot is already standing in a saucer or tray, fill this up and let the plant drink as much as it needs. However, remember to throw away any excess water still in the saucer as you do not want the plant to stay in it for extended periods – this can cause the plant to rot.

Plunging

Almost like a spa day for your plant, submerge the pot – but not the entire plant – into a bucket or sink full of water until the soil is moist, then allow any excess water to drain away before returning the plant pot to its outer pot or drip tray.

Bromeliad watering (fig.3, above)

Bromeliaceae (bromeliads), which form rosettes of leaves and grow brightly coloured bracts (leaves that look like flower petals) must be watered in a special way. The formation of this type of leaves creates a little cup or well around the plant's stem. The cup can be right at the top of the plant or further towards

the bottom and must be kept topped up with water. However, it is a good idea to empty the old water and refill the cup with fresh water every couple of months – just carefully tilt the plant until the old water pours out.

Use a small watering can to direct water into the cup; if you are not sure where the cup is on your bromeliad then dribble the water down the plant's stem from the very top and the water will naturally collect in the cup. Bromeliads absorb their nutrients through their leaves, so you also need to mist the plant regularly.

Holiday watering

We all go on holiday now and then, and we don't want our plants to suffer while we are away. Ideally, it's best to get someone to look after your plants while you're away, but sometimes this isn't possible. However, there are ways to give your plants some extra TLC while you're gone – here are a few techniques that could help:

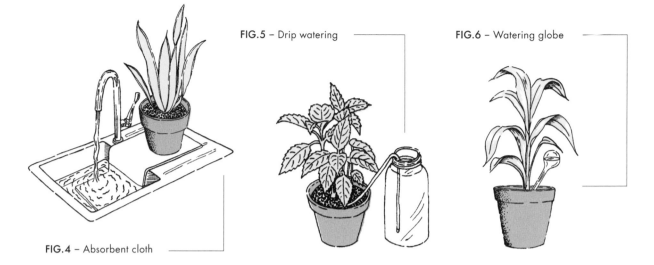

FIG.5 – Drip watering

FIG.6 – Watering globe

FIG.4 – Absorbent cloth

Absorbent cloth (fig. 4, above)

Fill the kitchen sink with cold water and lay a large absorbent cloth over the draining board so that it drapes into the water – make sure the cloth reaches the bottom of the sink. Place your plants onto the cloth on the draining board. The water will soak up the cloth and the plants will absorb the water from the cloth. Just don't forget to turn off the tap!

Drip watering (fig.5, above)

Fill a bottle with fresh water and stand it next to your plant. Cut a piece of string long enough so that one end dangles into the bottom of the bottle of water and the other end reaches the plant pot; push this end about 2 cm (¾ in) into the compost. The string will soak up the water and drip into the plant.

Watering globe (fig.6, above)

Watering globes are glass or plastic dibbers with a bulb at one end that you fill with water.

You then push the dibber into the compost. When the plant requires water, the compost pushes an air bubble up into the dibber and water comes out. Simple! This is also a system that can be used permanently for super needy ferns if you are a little forgetful. You can also buy a self-watering planter – though they are not a cheap option.

Feeding

Newly potted and repotted plants will have been planted in fresh compost, which is full of nutrients. However, over time these are used up by the plant and gradually washed away by watering, so house plants need an occasional feed using fertiliser. Liquid fertilisers are usually sold in concentrated form, so be careful to dilute them correctly so that you do not overfeed your plants – follow the maker's instructions properly.

You can also use slow-release granules, which you can put in the potting compost, but, if in doubt, check the manufacturer's instructions.

HOW TO SPOT THE EARLY SIGNS OF PLANT TROUBLES

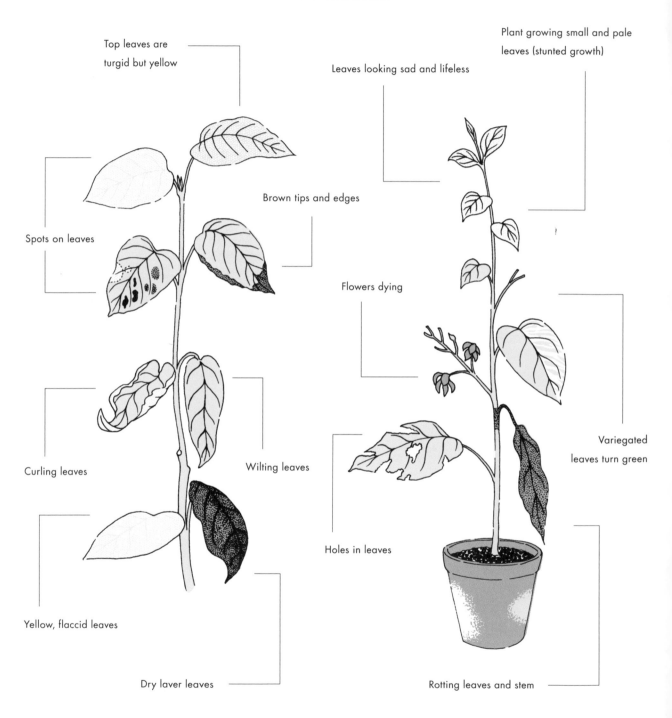

Top leaves are turgid but yellow

Plant growing small and pale leaves (stunted growth)

Leaves looking sad and lifeless

Brown tips and edges

Spots on leaves

Flowers dying

Curling leaves

Wilting leaves

Variegated leaves turn green

Yellow, flaccid leaves

Holes in leaves

Dry laver leaves

Rotting leaves and stem

PLANT TROUBLES & CULTURAL FAULTS

Sometimes your plants will start to have problems, but keep a watchful eye and observe your plants so you can spot any signs of trouble as early as possible – prevention is always better than cure.

Recognising Plant Troubles

Upper leaves turn yellow
This often happens when plants have been watered with hard tap water. Swap this for rain water or filtered tap water.

Brown spots & patches on leaves
If crisp, brown spots or patches appear on a plant's leaves, it has most likely been underwatered. However, if the spots are soft and dark brown the plant has probably been overwatered. So make sure you check the leaves carefully! It's vital you do not let the plant's compost completely dry out before you water it again, or that you do not water it when the compost is still moist from the last watering.

It is a fine balance to get watering right, but once you do the patches will no longer appear.

Brown leaves
If the entire leaf is brown, it could be due to over- or underwatering or too little or too much sun. Check that the plant is kept in the correct conditions (see page 47). If the leaves are brown in the middle this could be due to dry air, which you can fix by regularly misting to increase the humidity.

Leaves curling at the edges or dropping off
If the leaves on your plant start to curl or fall off, it has either been slightly overwatered or is not warm enough, perhaps because it is next to a cold draught. Move your plant to a more suitable area in your home.

Wilting leaves

If a plant's leaves start to wilt it is a sign of either underwatering or overwatering. However, if you are sure that watering is not the issue, the wilting may be caused by vine weevil grubs, which feed on roots. If you find a bad infestation, throw away the whole plant immediately.

Sudden leaf fall

Single leaves fall off plants all the time, but if many or all of the leaves fall off then the plant has had a shock, due either to exposure to extreme cold or heat, or from complete dehydration. It could also be movement shock; if a plant gets moved around a lot, this can shock it and cause sudden and total leaf fall. If this happens to your plant, leave it in a bright, warm space to give it a chance to recover. Dilute some fertiliser and feed the plant in a week's time. Don't move the plant again for at least a month.

Lower leaves dry up and fall

Usually this is caused by one of three things: the plant is not getting enough light; the plant is not warm enough; or you are underwatering your plant. Check that the light and heat levels in the place the plant lives are suited to that type of plant; if not, move the plant to a more suitable spot. If the light and temperature are right for the plant, make sure you are watering it before the compost gets too dry – if you are regularly letting it completely dry out before you water it again, the plant is getting too dehydrated. Use a self-watering pot or water globe to ensure the plant is getting enough moisture – but allow the plant to dry out first.

Holes in leaves

Believe it or not, holes in the leaves of indoor plants are not cause by insects or bugs. They are usually due to poor nutrition or excessive dry air. Try misting your plant with water to increase humidity levels.

Small, pale leaves (stunted growth)

If your plant starts to produce small, pale yellow leaves, this is could be due to a number of factors: poor drainage or light conditions or low humidity. Repot the plant (pages 112–113) or you could try aerating the soil. It is also worth moving your plant to a well-lit room or space.

Flowers dying

If your plant is failing to flower, it's likely to need more light or a boost of organic fertiliser. It's also worth checking for draughts. Try misting your plant with water to increase humidity levels.

If all else fails...

If you are having real trouble with your plants and you have exhausted some or all of my suggestions, here are three helpful tips you should follow:

1. Leave the plant to dry out slightly.
2. Make sure it has enough light.
3. Feed the plant some organic fertiliser.

HOW TO REVIVE A WILTED PLANT

If your plant has wilted, don't despair – you may be able to bring it back to life with these tips.

Leaves are wilting and dropping – this is because the plant is not getting enough water

The soil could have lost its ability to retain water

The roots could have shrunk, so the water drains straight out

Soak the plant in a bucket of water and spray with a mister

Break up the topsoil

Let the excess water drain. If the plant wilts again, repot in new soil

PROPAGATION & CUTTINGS

Growing plants indoors (and outdoors) is such a satisfying experience. One of the best things about keeping plants is that you can easily propagate (breed or grow) your own from scratch by simply taking cuttings.

Spider plants are great to propogate and produce babies quickly

Most plants have the incredible ability to duplicate themselves, and by simply taking a leaf or stem cutting you can create a whole new plant. Succulents are by far one of the easiest plants to propagate, which is great as they can sometimes be quite expensive to buy. To propagate leafier house plants, such as the spider plant, I would recommend taking a cutting from the leaf with some new shoots coming through, and cutting down as close to the root as possible. Leave the cuttings to dry for 24 hours, then place in a cup of water until the new shoots pop out (at least 4 days). Plant into its own pot using multipurpose compost.

HOW TO TAKE CUTTINGS FROM A SUCCULENT

1. Use a sharp knife or scissors to cut a leaf from the succulent – get as close as you can to the stem

3. If the leaf is short – lay it on top of some multi-purpose soil in a pot. But, if the leaf is longer, you can root and plant it standing up in the pot

2. Leave to dry out for a day

HOW TO TAKE CUTTINGS FROM A CACTUS

Use gloves and tongs
to remove the cutting

Try and get as much root as possible. Leave
the cutting for a day to dry out before potting

Opuntia microdasys (bunny ears) are great to
propogate – hold the 'ear' with tongs and cut
along the base of the jar to the main plant.
Careful – they are spiky

Use cactus soil and plant the
cutting on the top using tongs

MAKE AN OPEN TERRARIUM

Unlike a closed terrarium, which is completely sealed, an open terrarium is, as the name implies, left open. Desert plants like cacti and succulents are great for this sort of terrarium as they need more oxygen and do not like to be as humid and wet as they would be inside a closed terrarium.

Because open terrariums are not self-sustaining, I recommend lightly spraying the plants once a week with a mister. Please do not be tempted to pour water into your terrarium, as this may cause the plants to rot. Succulents and cacti like bright light, so it's best to keep your finished terrarium near a window.

At geo-fleur, we love geometric shapes and like to make terrariums in geometric glass containers. You can hunt for a vintage one or buy them in most gift stores or online. Alternatively, be creative with the vessel you use. Try making an open terrarium in an apothecary jar, large antique drinking glass or a fishbowl.

YOU WILL NEED

cactus potting compost

clear glass container or terrarium

activated charcoal

long-handled teaspoon

selection of small cacti and/or succulents

thin kitchen tongs

aquatic gravel (available at pet shops)

funnel (optional)

small paint brush

1. Spoon the potting compost into the bottom of the terrarium to a depth of about 5 cm (2 in).

2. Sprinkle a little bit of activated charcoal over the top of the compost.

3. If you can reach inside the container, use two fingers to make a well for your cactus or succulent to sit in; if you cannot use your fingers, use a long-handled spoon instead. Make sure you do not make the well too deep – you need to leave about 2 cm (¾ in) of soil at the bottom of the well.

4. Remove a plant from its pot – make sure you use the tongs to hold the plant if it is a cactus so you do not get spikes in your fingers. Gently squeeze the plastic pot that the plant is in and it should come out easily. If it is pot-bound – when the plant's roots fill the pot and start to grow out of the drainage holes – and will not come out, tickle the bottom of the pot to release the roots.

5. Holding the plant with tongs, angle it into the terrarium and place it into the well. If you find it difficult to hold the plant just using tongs, a little tip is to use your spoon and tongs like a knife and fork. Use the spoon or tongs to compress the soil around the plant to make sure it is nice and secure – you will probably need to spoon some more compost around the plant and compress it to achieve this. Make sure that the plant is not wobbling around.

6. Repeat steps 3–5 until all the plants are inside your terrarium. Use the top of your spoon to test if all the plants are secure by doing a wobble test: gently tap the top of the plant or nudge its leaves to see if it moves. If any are not firmly in place, add more compost and compress it around the plant.

7. Use the spoon to add a 2–3 cm (¾–1 in) layer of aquatic gravel on top of the compost. Please do not be tempted to add decorative stones instead, as the aquatic gravel helps with drainage. You can use a funnel instead of a spoon if this is easier or if your terrarium is a difficult shape.

8. If you get any of the gravel or soil on your plants, use the paint brush to dust off the debris.

Tag your finished #LivingWithPlantsTerrarium #LivingWithPlantsHowTo @geo_fleur

CHAPTER FIVE

PLANT STYLING

PLANT STYLING

It is important to think about where you will place your plants in your home: you do not want to overcrowd your plants as they need room to grow, but at the same time you do not want them looking lonely. Do you have a bright, sunny windowsill that is a little bare? Perhaps place *Monstera deliciosa* (Swiss cheese plant) cuttings along it to add some quick greenery as they are rapid growers when in the right environment. See page 144 for more inspiration on dressing your windowsill.

Plants tend to thrive when they are together, so it is nice to create a plant area made up of different sized and shaped pots and plants. Again, a windowsill is a good spot for this, but you can put a little plant gang virtually anywhere – just make sure the plants you choose are suited for that space (pages 21–24 and 47).

A key way to pick out different plants that look good together is to look for different shapes and textures that complement each other; for example, do not put brash, clashing bromeliads together, unless you are going for a rainbow effect. It is nice to pick out a blue-grey tone from a *Philodendron hastatum* (spade-leaf philodendron) and match it with a *Euphorbia lac-tea* (white ghost cactus) and a *Davallia canariensis* (hare's foot fern), as the colours work harmoniously together.

The rest of this chapter will show you various ways you can style your plants – whether by simply switching up the types of pot you use, or by displaying your plants in more ambitious ways.

How to: Arrange plants as table decorations

When you are entertaining, it is nice to decorate your table with some greenery. Depending on how much time and space you have, you can create a beautiful yet simple look with potted plants, or you can really go for it and make more extravagant holders to display your foliage.

Here are some ideas for you to try:

1. Set an odd number of different but complementary plants in pretty pots running in a straight line down the middle of the table. If you do not have much space down the centre of your table you can use mini potted plants – perhaps some mini cacti or succulents – then cut some stems of foliage from your garden and lay those on the table beside the pots. Alternatively, place a large planter in the centre of the table and decorate around it with smaller mini pots.

2. Make macramé plant hangers to hang over your table at various heights – see pages 35–39 for how to make them. This is great if you have high ceilings as it creates a dramatic effect. Hang trailing plants such as *Rhipsalis baccifera* (mistletoe cactus) and *Ceropegia woodii* (string of hearts) together and enjoy their different textures and leaf shapes.

3. Create a box of plants using a vintage crate, wardrobe or another interesting large container. Fill it with a variety of different but complementary plants – you can use the plants that you already own, so this is great for a low-budget option. Try to use a lot of different textures in the crate: I like to use a combination of ferns,

Tillandsia xerographica, *Pilea peperomioides* (Chinese money plant), *Sempervivums* (houseleeks), succulents, cacti and a mini *Crassula ovata* (jade plant). (See picture opposite.)

How to: create a #PlantShelfie

I am a big fan of *#PlantShelfies* on Instagram. All you need to do is arrange a gorgeous collection of plants on a shelf, then take a photo to show them off! They are pretty easy to replicate as you just need some shelf space to decorate. If you want to get some shelves especially for your *#PlantShelfie* you could use anything from simple Ikea picture rail shelving to something more stylised. Sticking to the Scandinavian theme, take a look at String shelving, created by iconic Swedish designer Nils Strinning, or family-run Danish company Woud.

Before you start, it is important to establish what kind of plants you want for your *#PlantShelfie*,

as it is better to have hardy plants on the top shelf so you do not have to water them as much. I would recommend some cacti on the top shelf and perhaps a *Tillandsia xerographica*, which you can easily lift down and water rather than climbing up to it. If height is not such an issue it is nice to use some trailing plants, such as *Ceropegia woodii* (string of hearts), which looks beautiful on a top shelf as its leaves dangle down.

On the lower shelves, which are easily accessible, you can add plants that need a bit more care such as some *Fittonia* (nerve plant). These will add a great pop of colour and you can use a few different varieties so that you have different shades of green, pinks and purples.

Depending on the length of your shelves, always try to have an odd number of plants on each one, as odd numbers tend to look better. You can also add some other accessories around the pots, like some ornaments – minimal Scandinavian-inspired objects are my personal choice, perhaps some

geometric shapes with some brass or copper. It's a great way to showcase your personality and put plants alongside the things you treasure most.

On the #PlantShelfie in my shop we have some vintage letter boards, which we use for plant identification and pricing, but at home you can write little messages to your friends or family. I also love plant puns!

How to: Top 5 easy plants to start your plant family

These plants look amazing when they're grouped together – the perfect starting point for your first plant shelfie.

1. *Spathiphyllum* (peace lily)
2. *Epipremnum aureum* (devil's ivy/golden pothos)
3. *Sansevieria trifasciata* (snake plant)
4. *Chlorophytum comosum* (spider plant)
5. *Aloe asphodelaceae* (aloe)

How to: dress a windowsill on a budget

Windowsills are one of the most popular and easiest places in a home to keep house plants, and dressing them well can make such a big difference to the room. One of the most important things to consider before choosing your plants is the direction your window is facing, as this will influence which plants you can keep on that windowsill – see page 47 for guidance.

If you do not have a lot of money to spend on plants it is great to start growing your collection with cuttings, particularly those from plants that propagate easily and grow very quickly – it will be very satisfying and you will get quick results. See pages 132–133 to learn how to take cuttings from different plants and how to propagate them. It is nice to ask friends if they have plants that you could take cuttings from, but if that is not possible then sometimes garden centres or nurseries sell cuttings much more cheaply than the fully-grown plant.

MAKE A LEATHER & BRASS PLANT HANGER

YOU WILL NEED

ruler

1.08 m (3 ft 6 in) of 3 cm- (1¼ in-)
    diameter copper or brass piping

hacksaw

cutting mat

rotary cutter

approx. 7.5 × 40 cm (3 × 16 in) piece of leather

leather hole puncher

spool of 1 mm-thick copper wire

wire cutters

copper plumbing Tee joint

superglue

gloves (optional)

This hanger is perfect for a succulent or *Rhipsalis* in a pot. You can hang the plant hanger from a picture hook or an S hook attached to a window ledge or curtain pole.

Use brass or copper piping depending on the look you prefer. You can find offcuts of leather from leather shoe shops or makers – choose any type or colour you like.

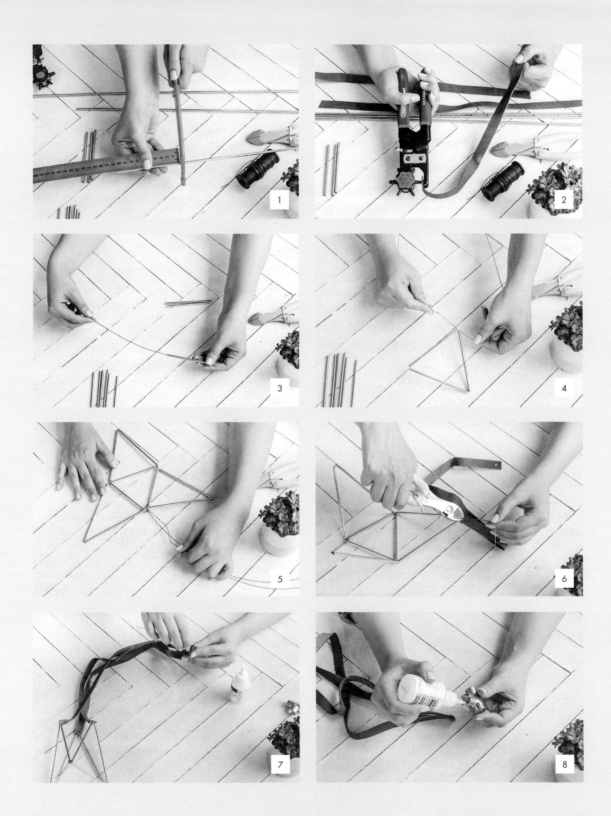

1. Use a ruler to mark out 3 × 10 cm (4 in) lengths of piping and cut them using the hacksaw. Then measure and cut 6 × 13 cm (5 in) lengths of piping.

2. Use a cutting mat and rotary cutter to cut 3 strips of leather measuring around 2.5 cm (3 in) wide and 30–40 cm (12–16 in) long.

3. With the leather hole puncher, punch a hole around 3 mm in diameter at each end of the strips of leather, about 1 cm (½ in) from the end of each strip. Do not make the holes too close to the ends of the strips, to avoid any risk of tearing.

4. Cut a 2 m (6 ft 7 in) length of copper wire using the wire cutters.

5. Thread the shorter pieces of piping onto the copper wire so that there is roughly 1.5 m (5 ft) of wire free at one end of the row of piping. Be careful, as the edges of the piping and wire are sharp. Fold the pipes at the joints to form a triangle and twist the wire together at the joint to keep it in place. This triangle will form the base of the holder and the bottom edges of 3 slightly longer triangles, which will form the sides.

6. Take the long side of the loose wire and thread on 2 of the longer pieces of piping. Fold these 2 pieces over at their joint to make another triangle, the third side being one edge of the base triangle. Twist the wire around the joint where the longer pipe meets the corner of the shorter triangle to secure them together. You will now have one smaller triangle with another taller triangle coming off one side.

7. Continuing with the same piece of wire, thread on 2 more of the longer pieces of triangle. Again, fold them at the joint and secure the end at the next corner joint of the original triangle. You will now have the original smaller triangle and 2 smaller triangles. Thread and secure the final 2 pieces of piping in the same way so that the

smaller base triangle now has 3 taller triangles attached to it. Make sure that the wire is secure at the last joint by wrapping it several times to ensure that it will not come undone and the piping will stay fixed.

8. Make sure that all the pieces are equal, then fold them up to a point to make a triangular pyramid. Cut the ends off the wire from the joint.

9. Cut a 15 cm (6 in) piece of copper wire and thread it through one of the holes in the end of one of the straps of leather. Join the end of the leather strap to the top of one of the tall triangles at the joint – it is almost like sewing with a needle and thread. Wrap the wire around the leather hole and the triangle joint 4–5 times to make sure it is secure, then cut off the excess wire and fold the remaining ends under – be careful as they could be sharp.

10. Repeat step 9 for the remaining leather straps, until all 3 are attached to the piping.

11. Flatten the 3 leather straps and join them at the top through the other holes with a 10 cm (4 in) piece of copper wire by 'sewing' them together.

12. Line the inside edge of the vertical stem part of the tee joint with superglue – be careful that you do not stick yourself to anything! It is a good idea to use gloves for this step. Push the end of the sewn-together pieces of leather into the tee joint. Make sure that the superglue does not seep out onto the leather – if it does, use a wet cloth to wipe it off.

13. Leave the hanger to dry for about 2 hours to let the superglue set before putting your plant inside and hanging wherever you choose.

Tag your finished #LivingWithPlantsPlantHanger #LivingWithPlantsHowTo @geo_fleur

MAGIC PLANT SECRETS

Here I share a few magic plant secrets and tricks,
to sum up my best plant wisdom!

1. The most common mistake is to overwater your plants. Keep the soil moist by misting every now and then but only re-water when it has almost dried out – when in doubt, leave it be!

2. Take cuttings from friends' plants – it's the best way to grow your collection.

3. If space is limited try using tall, narrow pots so that minimal floor space is taken up, or even invest in small plants such as succulents and cacti. Hanging plants from windowsills in macramé baskets is a great space-saver too!

4. Group your plants together in odd numbers – they grow better when they are with their friends.

5. Plants need time to acclimatise to new environments. Therefore, try not to relocate them too frequently as this may cause them to wilt.

6. Keep plants healthy by regularly pruning them. Pinch off any dying flowers or yellowing leaves, and, if necessary, cut any wayward branches.

What a journey it has been: the beginning of geo-fleur has been such a great rollercoaster – and we can't wait to show you everything else we have in store! I hope you have learned some valuable tips from my book, that it has inspired you to start your own *#plantgang*, and that you now know how to maintain your collection of plants and help them thrive. We also host workshops at geo-fleur, which are a great way to learn more about your plants and socialise with friends. You can keep up with what I'm up to via Instagram: @geo_fleur

Enjoy!

PLANT INDEX

This is the magic place to come to check what plants you could have, and how to keep them happy and cared for. For more advice on the different watering techniques that are mentioned here see pages 124–127.

Warning: Some plants are toxic to pets. If you have pets, always check the plant label or ask your shop or gardening centre before introducing plants to your home.

A

Adiantum (maidenhair fern)

These are rather needy plants. Keep their compost moist at all times and mist the leaves regularly when looking dry (pages 82, 85, 116).

Aeonium

These succulents bear rosettes of leaves ranging in colour from yellow to almost black. The rosettes may be flat saucers of densely packed leaves, as in the Aeonium tabuliforme (flat-topped aeonium), or a looser arrangement on the top of branches as found on Aeonium arboretum (houseleek tree).

Aloe asphodelaceae (aloe vera)

Water your aloe vera from the bottom and allow the compost to dry out before watering again. Very easy to propagate and will have lots of 'babies' (pages 42, 143).

Ananas bracteatus (red pineapple)

This impressive looking plant produces red pineapples and is a member of the Bromeliaceae family, commonly called bromeliads. Water it down its stem like other bromeliads (page 88).

Asparagus aethiopicus (Sprenger's asparagus)

Water from the bottom and keep warm. Mist to increase humidity (page 82, 85).

Asplenium nidus (bird's nest fern)

Water from the bottom and mist to increase humidity.

B

Bromeliaceae (bromeliad)

Water down its stem (pages 24, 87, 102).

C

Calathea orbifolia (zebra plant)

Water from the bottom and mist regularly.

Chlorophytum comosum (spider plant)

Keep them well watered from the bottom and mist regularly (pages 49, 50, 143).

Crassula ovata (jade plant/money tree)

Water from the bottom or spray weekly – treat like a succulent (page 142).

Crassula arborescens (silver dollar plant)

Treat like a succulent – water from the bottom or spray weekly.

Crassula perforata (string of buttons)

Mist every two weeks – be careful as can go mouldy very quickly.

Calathea roseopicta (rose-painted calathea)

Water from the bottom and mist weekly (page 24).

D

Davallia (hare's foot fern)

These plants have weird furry 'feet' that the fern leaves grow out of. Water from the bottom and mist weekly (pages 25, 141).

E

Echeveria agavoides 'Multifera'
(moulded wax plant)

Treat like a succulent – water from the bottom or spray weekly.

Echeveria lilacina (ghost echeveria)

Mist weekly: treat like a succulent.

Echeveria halbingeri

Treat like a succulent – water from the bottom or spray weekly.

Echinocactus grusonii (barrel cactus)

Water fortnightly from the bottom.

F

Ficus elastica (rubber tree)

Water from the bottom and mist every week (page 33).

Ficus lyrata (fiddle leaf fig)

Water from the bottom and mist weekly. Keep warm (pages 8, 25).

Fittonia albinvenis (nerve plant)

Water from the bottom and keep the compost moist. Mist three times a week and if the leaves wilt it needs watering more frequently. Sometimes called a silver net plant (pages 47, 116, 119, 143).

H

Haworthia fasciata (zebra cactus)

The zebra cactus is an aloe-like succulent, which bears thick and warty leaves. Very hardy; spray with water weekly.

M

Monstera deliciosa (Swiss cheese plant)

Water from the bottom and spray weekly; its leaves will go floppy if it is not getting enough water (pages 19, 23, 24, 49, 111, 141.

Musa (banana palm)

Very hardy. Water from the bottom and mist for humidity.

O

Opuntia microdasys (bunny ear cactus)

Mist weekly.

P

Philodendron

Water from the bottom and water weekly; its leaves will go soft if it is not getting enough water. However, be sure not to overwater (pages 23, 141).

Phlebodium pseudoaureum
(blue rabbit's foot fern)

Keep moist, water from the bottom and mist to increase humidity.

Pilea peperomioides (Chinese money plant)

Leaves and stalks will go floppy and soft if it is not getting

enough water; water from the bottom and mist. Very easy to propagate (pages 24, 25, 47, 142).

Platycerium (staghorn fern)

Water from the bottom and mist the leaves; if its leaves are floppy it needs more water.

S

Sedum morganianum (burro's tail)

Mist weekly – do not allow it to get too wet as it will go mouldy.

Sempervivum tectorum (common houseleek)

Sempervivum is an old favourite both indoors and out. They are completely hardy – they seem to thrive on neglect and should not be overwatered, overfed or repotted unnecessarily (pages 75, 142).

Senecio rowleyanus (string of pearls)

This group of Senecios is strange indeed; pendant threads bearing bead-like leaves.

Strelitzia reginae (bird of paradise)

The bird of paradise usually flowers in spring, but sometimes does so earlier or later. Surely the most spectacular of all the flowers which can be grown in the home. The vivid flowers can last for several weeks on top of tall stalks, surrounded by large leaves. It need patience – new plants take four to six years before flowering – and space. Tricks to encourage it to flower: it loves average warmth, as much as light as possible, being watered thoroughly, then leave until the compost surface is dry. Water sparingly in winter.

T

Tillandsia (air plant)

Air plants have some great qualities and there are lots of different varieties. The basic rule is to care for them correctly: mist them two to three times a week, or submerge them in water for 10 minutes and then let them dry. The most common species are *Tillandsia ionantha* (sky plant) and *Tillandsia abdita* (pages 87, 88).

Tillandsia xerographica (xerographica)

A hardy air plant. Submerge it in water once a week and let it dry (pages 94, 142, 143).

BOOK INDEX

Page numbers in *italics* are illustrations

Thank Yous

A huge thank you to my mum, Sue: you are such an inspiration and I'd be lost without you. A huge thanks to Sally, who keeps me sane day-to-day with the logistics of our business – and we have the BEST fun doing it. Also, a big thanks to Leonie Freeman, who shot this book when she was 7 months pregnant. You are a super woman!

A big thanks to Kim Lucas, who was our talented hand model, and to Rowan Spray, who was our photography assistant and helped to keep us organised on shoots, lifting hundreds of plants in and out of locations. A huge thank you to all the team at Hardie Grant and Charlotte Heal for her beautiful book design. Thank you to Jacqueline Colley for her wonderful plant illustrations. And a thank you to Jovanna, who has kept me sane with her design and kind words. You are a wonderful lady.

About the Author

Sophie Lee studied Fine Art at Westminster University, but as her mum is a florist, she has always been surrounded with plants and greenery. She started geo-fleur in 2014, and has had roaring success ever since, with 80,000 followers on Instagram. She has worked with some very exciting clients such as Sweaty Betty, ASOS, and Liberty London. Sophie also styled plants for the Turner Prize at the Tate Britain. She has been featured in *The Sunday Times*, *Elle Decoration*, *Stylist* and the *Telegraph*.

She lives in London, with a house full of plants.

Living with Plants by Sophie Lee

First published in 2017 by Hardie Grant Books

Hardie Grant Books (UK)
52-54 Southwark Street
London SE1 1UN
hardiegrant.co.uk

Hardie Grant Books (Australia)
Ground Floor, Building 1
658 Church Street
Melbourne, VIC 3121
hardiegrant.com.au

British Library Cataloguing-in-Publication Data. A catalogue record
for this book is available from the British Library.

ISBN: 978-1-78488-096-5

Publisher: Kate Pollard
Commissioning Editor: Kajal Mistry
Editorial Assistant: Hannah Roberts
Publishing Assistant: Eila Purvis
Photographer: Leonie Freeman
Photography Assistant: Rowan Spray
Art Direction: CHD
Design Assistant: Chelsie Fleming
Cover Concept: Hardie Grant
Illustrations: Jaqueline Colley
Copy editor: Susan Pegg
Indexer: Cathy Heath
Colour Reproduction by p2d

Printed and bound in China by 1010

10 9 8 7 6 5 4 3 2 1